The Bibliography of Contemporary American Fiction, 1945-1988: An Annotated Checklist

MECKLER'S LITERARY BIBLIOGRAPHIES

Walker Percy: A Bibliography: 1930-1984
by Stuart Wright
ISBN 0-88736-046-7 CIP 1986

The Bibliography of Contemporary American
Poetry, 1945-1985: An Annotated Checklist
by William McPheron
ISBN 0-88736-054-8 CIP 1986

Harry Crews: A Bibliography
by Michael Hargraves
ISBN 0-88736-060-2 CIP 1986

William Goyen: A Descriptive Bibliography,
1938-1985
by Stuart Wright
ISBN 0-88736-057-2 CIP 1986

Stevie Smith: A Bibliography
by Jack Barbera, William McBrien
& Helen Bajan
ISBN 0-88736-101-3 CIP 1987

Sylvia Plath: An Analytical Bibliography
by Stephen Tabor
ISBN 0-88736-100-5 CIP 1987

H. Rider Haggard: A Bibliography
by D.E. Whatmore
ISBN 0-88736-102-1 CIP 1987

Robert Gover: A Descriptive Bibliography
by Michael Hargraves
ISBN 0-88736-165-X CIP 1988

Confederate Broadside Poems:
An Annotated Descriptive Bibliography
by William Moss
ISBN 0-88736-163-3 CIP 1988

Alice Malsenior Walker:
An Annotated Bibliography: 1968-1986
by Louis H. Pratt and Darnell D. Pratt
ISBN 0-88736-156-0 CIP 1988

Supplement to A Bibliography of
George Moore
by Edwin Gilcher
ISBN 0-88736-199-4 CIP 1988

Alan Sillitoe: A Bibliography
by David Gerard
ISBN 0-88736-104-8 CIP 1988

John Wain: A Bibliography
by David Gerard
ISBN 0-88736-103-X CIP 1988

The Making of the Shelley Myth:
An Annotated Bibliography of Criticism of
P.B. Shelley, 1822-1860
by Karsten Klejs Engelberg
ISBN 0-88736-298-2 CIP 1988

PKD: A Philip K. Dick Bibliography,
Revised Edition
by Daniel J. H. Levack and Steven Owen
Godersky
ISBN 0-88736-096-3 CIP 1988

Dune Master: A Frank Herbert
Bibliography
by Daniel J. H. Levack and Mark Willard
ISBN 0-88736-099-8 CIP 1988

Gothic Fiction: A Master List of
Twentieth Century Criticism
and Research
by Frederick S. Frank
ISBN 0-88736-218-4 CIP 1988

The Bibliography of Contemporary
American Fiction, 1945-1988:
An Annotated Checklist
by William McPheron and
Jocelyn Sheppard
ISBN 0-88736-167-6 CIP 1989

Robinson Crusoe: An Annotated
Checklist of English Language Editions,
1719-1985
by Robert Lovett
ISBN 0-88736-058-0 CIP *forthcoming*

Donald Davie: A Descriptive Bibliography
by Stuart Wright
ISBN 0-88736-059-9 CIP *forthcoming*

John Ciardi: A Descriptive Bibliography
by Charles C. Lovett and
Stephanie B. Lovett
ISBN 0-88736-056-4 CIP *forthcoming*

Lewis Carroll's Alice: An Annotated
Checklist of Editions in English
by Charles C. Lovett and
Stephanie B. Lovett
ISBN 0-88736-166-8 CIP *forthcoming*

Robert Lowell: A Descriptive
Bibliography
by Stephen Gould Axelrod
ISBN 0-88736-227-3 CIP *forthcoming*

James Tate: A Descriptive Bibliography
by Gene DeGruson
ISBN 0-88736-229-X CIP *forthcoming*

Richard Eberhart: A Descriptive
Bibliography
by Stuart Wright
ISBN 0-88736-346-6 CIP *forthcoming*

Clifford Odets: An Annotated
Bibliography of Criticism
by Robert Cooperman
ISBN 0-88736-326-1 CIP *forthcoming*

The Bibliography of Contemporary American Fiction, 1945-1988: An Annotated Checklist

William McPheron
and
Jocelyn Sheppard

Meckler
Westport • London

Library of Congress Cataloging-in-Publication Data

McPheron, William
    The bibliography of contemporary American fiction, 1945-1988

    Includes Index.
    1. American fiction--20th century--History and criticism--Bibliography.
2. Bibliography--Bibliography--American fiction. I. Sheppard, Jocelyn. II.
Title.
Z1231.F4M36 1989 [PS379] 016.813'54'09 88-13522
ISBN 0-88736-167-6 (alk. paper)

British Cataloging in Publication Data

McPheron, William
    The bibliography of contemporary American fiction, 1945-1988 : an
annotated checklist. 1. Fiction in English. American writers, 1945 --
Bibliographies I. Title II. Sheppard, Jocelyn
016.813'54'08
ISBN 0-88736-167-6

Meckler Corporation, 11 Ferry Lane West, Westport, CT 06880.
Meckler Ltd., Grosvenor Gardens House, Grosvenor Gardens,
    London SW1W 0BS, U.K.

Printed on acid free paper.
Printed and bound in the United States of America.

Contents

Preface

This checklist records and describes bibliographical accounts of contemporary American fiction writers, with emphasis on single-author studies. The volume's purposes are several: to trace the historical development of the bibliography of individual writers, to indicate the depth of bibliographical treatment of those writers currently available to scholars and librarians, and finally to highlight the need for additional bibliographical research in the field.

The multi-author section is organized alphabetically by author or editor, except when these are lacking, in which instance entry is by title. Focus here is on reference tools that provide substantial coverage of individual novelists and short story writers. Excluded are the numerous serial bibliographies and periodical indexes which furnish access to the primary and secondary materials of the field but do not feature significant single-author compilations. Also omitted from this section are both out-of-date tools whose bibliographical information has been incorporated in more recent works as well as the many selective guides to genre fiction that propose to list the best, or most important books within their different areas of concentration. Emphasis lies, in short, on current reference tools whose bibliographical accounts of individual fiction writers comprehend a variety of sources and consequently represent a useful addition to the author's total bibliography.

The single-author section concentrates on writers of adult fiction whose reputations have been established since 1945. Though authors of children's literature are omitted, this volume's scope does extend beyond the boundaries of mainstream commercial fiction to include practitioners of the genres of science fiction and fantasy, detective, crime, mystery, and historical fiction as well as regional, ethnic, and small press writers. Poets whose fiction is essentially incidental to their literary reputations are not represented--hence the absence of figures like Robert Creeley, James Dickey, and Robert Kelly. (Each of these as well as other poets who occasionally write fiction are fully treated in William McPheron's *The Bibliography of Contemporary American Poetry, 1945-1985*. Meckler, 1986.) Authors whose fiction constitutes an integral dimension of an otherwise multi-faceted career are, however, treated fully, so that coverage of such writers as Charles Bukowski, Jim Harrison, and George Garrett is provided. Also included are a few writers who emerged into prominence prior to 1945 but whose continued production of new work maintained their presence on the contemporary publishing scene into the late 1970s. Peter De Vries, Isaac Bashevis Singer, and Robert Penn Warren exemplify this small group.

Entries under the fiction writers' names in the single-author section are arranged chronologically, then alphabetically by compiler within the year. Only bibliographically serious accounts are recorded. Highly selective checklists routinely appearing in critical monographs or printed in issues of journals specially devoted to a writer have been excluded, except in a few cases where no other coverage is available. Bibliographies appended to unpublished doctoral dissertations, and theses that are full-scale bibliographical studies, have been identified. Within these limits, the checklist is intended to be complete through 1986, but with references to as many 1987 and 1988 publications as possible.

The descriptions are based on first-hand examination, except those entries indicated by an asterisk (*). For these unseen references, sources of citation are supplied. Most of them are bibliographical studies that were published privately for limited audiences and in limited editions or that appeared in special interest magazines. In this regard, science fiction fanzines and several new French journals devoted to American crime fiction proved particularly difficult to obtain and, in fact, account for most of our asterisked entries.

We also want to express our appreciation for the considerate assistance of our respective institutions' interlibrary loan services, most particularly

Sonia H. Moss of the Stanford University Libraries and Anne E. Clifford of SUNY/Buffalo's Lockwood Memorial Library.

Stanford University   William McPheron
State University of New York at Buffalo   Jocelyn Sheppard
June 1988

3

Multi-Author Studies

1. Adelman, Irving, and Rita Dworkin. *The Contemporary Novel: A Checklist of Critical Literature on the British and American Novel Since 1945*. Metuchen, N.J.: Scarecrow Press, 1972.

   Selective, unannotated coverage of the secondary journal literature to 1968 and of critical books through 1969. Though writers whose careers began prior to 1945 are included if they were productive or first recognized after World War II, many truly contemporary figures are included. Emphasis is on the more significant writings about an author and includes reviews when appropriate.

2. Albert, Walter. *Detective and Mystery Fiction: An International Bibliography of Secondary Sources*. Madison, Ind.: Brownstone Books, 1985.

   Exhaustive international checklist of the critical and scholarly writings on crime, mystery, suspense, and espionage fiction, excluding only Sherlockian literature. Largest section is devoted to studies of individual authors, many of whom are contemporary American practitioners of those genres. All entries are fully annotated.

3. Anderson, John O., Edwin W. Gaston, Jr., and James W. Lee, eds. *Southwestern American Literature: A Bibliography*. Chicago: Swallow Press, 1980.

The second half of this reference tool consists of checklists of Southwestern authors, many of whom are contemporary novelists and short story writers. Bibliographical coverage includes an enumerative record of books, a list of uncollected periodical contributions, and selected, unannotated secondary references, generally excluding reviews.

4.   Bleiler, E.F., ed. *Science Fiction Writers: Critical Studies of the Major Authors from the Early Nineteenth Century to the Present Day*. New York: Scribner's, 1982.

The two chapters devoted to contemporary writers, "The Circumbellum Period" and "The Moderns," occupy two-thirds of this one-volume reference tool and include many current American authors of science fiction. For each treated, a selective, enumerative list of book publications is furnished, followed by an unannotated record of major criticism, with book reviews generally excluded. Especially valuable for the few major writers not yet the subject of intense bibliographical scrutiny, such as Richard Matheson and Judith Merril.

5.   ----------. *Supernatural Fiction Writers: Fantasy and Horror*. 2 vols. New York: Scribner's, 1985.

Organized chronologically by period, this set features in its second volume two sections that treat contemporary American authors of supernatural fiction, "American Pulp Writers of the Circumbellum Period" and "British and American Modern Writers." For each author included, enumerative primary and unannotated secondary bibliographies are furnished. Both are selective but these checklists can be very useful in the cases of writers such as Patricia McKillip and Richard Matheson, for whom other substantial bibliographies are absent.

6.   Bruccoli, Matthew J., and Philip B. Eppard. *First Printings of American Authors: Contributions Toward Descriptive Checklists*. 5 vols. Detroit: Gale, 1977-1987.

Each alphabetically organized volume reviews a wide range of American authors, many of whom are contemporary novelists and short story writers. Provides for each a chronological record of separate publications wholly or substantially by the writer, with later printings or editions noted only when they incorporate new material or significant revisions. Books edited, translated, introduced, or otherwise containing important contributions are also listed. Though treatment of items is essentially enumerative, title pages of first editions are routinely reproduced and other critical elements of a title's publishing history are noted. Volume 5 concludes with an index to the entire set.

7. Colonnese, Tom, and Louis Owens. *American Indian Novelists: An Annotated Critical Bibliography*. Garland Reference Library of the Humanities 384. New York: Garland, 1985.

> Provides comprehensive coverage of the novels of twenty-one American Indians. All primary entries are accompanied by plot summaries, while secondary materials receive full contents notes. For each writer treated, only a broad selection of non-novelistic work is furnished. The contemporary figures included in the volume are Paula Gunn Allen, Denton R. Bedford, Dallas Chief Eagle, Janet Campbell Hale, Jamake Highwater, Markoosie, N. Scott Momaday, Nasnaga (Roger Russell), Chief George Pierre, Leslie Marmon Silko, Virginia Driving Hawk Sneve, Hyemeyhsts Storm, John William Tebbel, James Tucker, Gerald Vizenor, and James Welch.

8. *Contemporary Authors: A Bio-Bibliographical Guide to Current Writers in Fiction, General Nonfiction, Poetry, Journalism, Drama, Motion Pictures, Television, and Other Fields*. Detroit: Gale, 1962- . New Revision Series, 1981- .

> Furnishes enumerative checklists of books and a record of uncollected periodical contributions for an extremely wide range of contemporary English-language writers. Selective coverage of secondary references, both biographical and critical, is also provided. Entries for individual writers are often revised and

updated. The most recent *Contemporary Authors* volume always contains a comprehensive index to the entire series. Especially valuable because of the inclusion of minor, or newly emerging, writers not treated elsewhere.

9.   Cowart, David, and Thomas L. Wymer. *Twentieth-Century American Science Fiction Writers*. 2 vols. Dictionary of Literary Biography 8, Pts. 1-2. Detroit: Bruccoli Clark/Gale, 1981.

This two-volume reference tool offers selected bibliographical information for about ninety authors, the overwhelming majority of whose writing careers began since World War II. Primary coverage for each focuses on books and other separately published works, such as screenplays and collections of essays. Treatment of their contributions to periodicals is more limited, while the unannotated list of secondary sources is similarly restricted to more important items. The set is especially valuable for the many prominent science fiction writers who have not yet become subjects of bibliographical studies.

10.   Currey, L.W. *Science Fiction and Fantasy Authors: A Bibliography of First Printings of Their Fiction and Selected Nonfiction*. Boston: G.K. Hall, 1979.

Furnishes abbreviated descriptive treatment for the primary texts of over 200 English-language science fiction and fantasy authors, many of whom are contemporary American writers. Presents for each a complete record of all fiction and selected nonfiction published in book, pamphlet, and broadside format. Description of each item is sufficient to identify both the first printings and all other bibliographically significant editions. Biographical, critical, and bibliographical books concerning the writers are also recorded. Primary coverage extends through 1977; secondary through mid-1979. No references to periodical literature, either primary or secondary, are included.

11.   Davis, Thadious M., and Trudier Harris, eds. *Afro-American Fiction Writers after 1955*. Dictionary of Literary Biography 33. Detroit: Bruccoli Clark/Gale, 1984.

Provides basic bibliographic information about forty-nine Afro-American novelists and short story writers who have actively published since 1955. Enumerative primary coverage lists books, uncollected periodical articles, and interviews. Unannotated secondary coverage furnishes selected record of reviews and critical commentary. Especially valuable for writers whose popular and academic reputations have not yet achieved great prominence.

12. ----------. *Afro-American Writers after 1955: Dramatists and Prose Writers*. Dictionary of Literary Biography 38. Detroit: Bruccoli Clark/Gale, 1985.

Complements Item 11, treating some writers, such as Toni Cade Bambara, Calvin C. Hernton, and James Alan McPherson, whose careers are importantly involved with fiction.

13. *Dictionary of Literary Biography Yearbook*. Detroit: Bruccoli Clark/Gale, 1981- .

Beginning with coverage for 1980, this annual reviews the year's literary events, both updating earlier entries in the *Dictionary of Literary Biography* and also publishing new bio-bibliographical articles on writers who might have been included in earlier volumes but were omitted. Each annual supplement also contains an index to all preceding volumes in the series and should be consulted to ascertain the extent and currency of treatment provided by the *Dictionary* and its *Yearbook*.

14. Duke, Maurice, Jackson R. Bryer, and M. Thomas Inge, eds. *American Women Writers: Bibliographical Essays*. Westport, Ct.: Greenwood Press, 1983.

Included in this work's scope are four contemporary American fiction writers--Eudora Welty, Flannery O'Connor, Anais Nin, and Carson McCullers. For each, an essay evaluates the major primary and secondary sources, with separate sections that survey bibliographies, trace histories of editions, review holdings of manuscripts and other unpublished materials, and analyze both biographies and critical studies.

15. Eger, Ernestina N. *A Bibliography of Criticism of Contemporary Chicano Literature*. Berkeley: Chicano Studies Library Publications, University of California, 1982.

    The central and largest section of this volume offers an unannotated checklist of critical commentary on individual Chicano writers, many of whom are contemporary novelists. Eger also devotes a section to the general criticism of Mexican-American prose fiction. This extensive coverage of secondary references, which reaches into 1979, significantly supplements that furnished by Item 28.

16. Erisman, Fred, and Richard W. Etulain, eds. *Fifty Western Writers: A Bio-Bibliographical Sourcebook*. Westport, Ct.: Greenwood Press, 1982.

    Furnishes selective checklists of primary and secondary materials for numerous contemporary fiction writers associated with the American West, including Edward Abbey, Benjamin Capps, William Eastlake, A.B. Guthrie, Jr., Ken Kesey, Louis L'Amour, Larry McMurtry, N. Scott Momaday, Wright Morris, and Wallace Stegner. Each bibliography is preceded by a narrative survey of the criticism, which usefully summarizes the principal issues.

17. Fallon, Eileen. *Words of Love: A Complete Guide to Romance Fiction*. Garland Reference Library of the Humanities 382. New York: Garland, 1984.

    The bulk of this reference tool is occupied by two chapters, "Historically Important Writers" and "Current Romance Authors," which consist of alphabetically arranged, single-author bio-bibliographies. While some of the writers treated in the first chapter are contemporary, all in the second are current practitioners, and many in both categories are American. For all writers treated, basic biographical information is followed by an enumerative checklist of their novels, presented according to the type of romance.

18. Fairbanks, Carol, and Eugene A. Engeldinger. *Black American Fiction: A Bibliography*. Metuchen, N.J.: Scarecrow Press, 1978.

Offers checklists of works by and about a remarkably wide range of Afro-American novelists and short story writers, most of whom are contemporary. Enumerative primary coverage enters both separately published novels and contributions of fiction to periodicals. Unannotated secondary record includes biography and criticism along with extensive coverage of reviews. References extend into 1977. This tool is particularly important for its attention to numerous writers not treated elsewhere.

19. Flora, Joseph M., and Robert Bain, eds. *Fifty Southern Writers After 1900: A Bio-Bibliographical Sourcebook*. Westport, Ct.: Greenwood Press, 1987.

Presents highly selective checklists of works by and about such prominent contemporary fiction writers as John Barth, Doris Betts, Truman Capote, Harry Crews, Ralph Ellison, Shelby Foote, Ernest J. Gaines, Shirley Ann Grau, Carson McCullers, Flannery O'Connor, Walker Percy, Reynolds Price, Elizabeth Spencer, Jesse Stuart, William Styron, Peter Taylor, Anne Tyler, Robert Penn Warren, and Eudora Welty. The checklists are preceded by introductory essays that define governing themes and critical issues as they appear in the major works and principal criticism.

20. Helterman, Jeffrey, and Richard Layman. *American Novelists Since World War II*. Dictionary of Literary Biography 2. Detroit: Bruccoli Clark/Gale, 1978.

Provides basic bibliographical coverage for eighty writers who published their first novels after 1945 or whose most important work has been done since then. Enumerative checklist of separately issued books followed by selected, unannotated record of major critical commentary. Particularly important for writers not yet the subject of in-depth bibliographies.

21. Houston, Helen Ruth. *The Afro-American Novel, 1965-1975: A Descriptive Bibliography of Primary and Secondary Material.* Troy, N.Y.: Whitson, 1977.

Usefully annotated coverage of writings by and about fifty-six Afro-American novelists who published in the period 1965-1975. Primary scope extends to books and periodical articles; secondary treatment lists biographical and critical commentary as well as reviews of individual works. Only materials published within the decade are entered, but for every item, including the novels, a brief summary of plot or argument is furnished. Particularly valuable for its coverage of less well known writers and for its annotations.

22. Hubin, Allen J. *Crime Fiction, 1749-1980: A Comprehensive Bibliography.* Garland Reference Library of the Humanities 371; and *1981-1985 Supplement to Crime Fiction, 1749-1980.* Garland Reference Library of the Humanities 766. New York: Garland, 1984, 1988. Previous ed. 1979.

The Author Index occupies the bulk of these volumes, listing first American and British editions of book titles under the bylines associated with them, with cross references to other entries for that author. Treats numerous contemporary American writers, many of whom are covered neither individually nor in such comparable reference tools as Item 34. No references to periodical or secondary literature.

23. Kay, Mary Jane. *The Romantic Spirit: A Romance Bibliography of Authors and Titles.* San Antonio: MJK Enterprises, 1982. 1983-1984 supplement, San Antonio: MJK Enterprises, 1984.

Lists the titles published by approximately 5,000 romance authors and their various pseudonyms. Arranged in two sections: the first organized alphabetically by writers' names, the other by romance line (e.g., Harlequin). Not as consistently systematic as Item 48 but scope is broader. Emphasis is on contemporary figures.

24. Kibler, James E., Jr., ed. *American Novelists Since World War II: Second Series*. Dictionary of Literary Biography 6. Detroit: Bruccoli Clark/Gale, 1980.

   Complements Item 20, providing an identical level of bibliographical coverage for an additional seventy American novelists whose writing careers have developed since 1945 but who have received less widespread critical attention.

25. Lepper, Gary M. *A Bibliographical Introduction to 75 Modern American Authors*. Berkeley: Serendipity Books, 1976.

   Provides primary coverage of separate publications through 1975 for selected authors who have achieved prominence since 1945, including numerous fiction writers. Every entry lists individual books, scripts, and translations by the author, as well as such fugitive materials as broadsides and postcards. Each item is briefly described in its first edition as well as in all bibliographically significant, subsequent editions. This tool is particularly useful for its abbreviated descriptions of the works of many contemporary writers who have not yet received this level of bibliographic attention.

26. Margolies, Edward, and David Bakish. *Afro-American Fiction, 1853-1976: A Guide to Information Sources*. American Literature, English Literature, and World Literatures in English Information Guide Series 25. Detroit: Gale, 1979.

   Separate enumerative checklists of novels and short story collections, organized alphabetically by the writers' names, precedes annotated coverage of selected secondary studies of major Afro-American writers. The primary checklists are especially valuable for minor writers not treated elsewhere. The secondary section furnishes substantial but still limited coverage of criticism.

27. Martine, James J., ed. *American Novelists*. Vol. 1 of *Contemporary Authors Bibliographical Series*. Detroit: Bruccoli Clark/Gale, 1986.

Supplements its selective lists of works by and about major post-World War II American novelists with highly informative bibliographical essays that carefully summarize and evaluate the most important secondary references about each author. Writers treated include James Baldwin, John Barth, Saul Bellow, John Cheever, Joseph Heller, Norman Mailer, Bernard Malamud, Carson McCullers, John Updike, and Eudora Welty. Materials covered for each: bibliographies, biographies, interviews, books, and articles.

28. Martinez, Julio A., and Francisco A. Lomeli, eds. *Chicano Literature: A Reference Guide*. Westport, Ct.: Greenwood Press, 1985.

Provides basic primary and secondary bibliographical information for a wide range of contemporary Mexican-American fiction writers who publish in English. Enumerative lists of works by the authors focus on books, but some uncollected periodical items are regularly noted. Selective treatment of secondary references includes both critical essays and reviews. Because many of these writers are neglected by the general bibliographies concerned with contemporary fiction in English, this volume as well as Items 15 and 43 furnish much unique bibliographical coverage.

29. McCaffery, Larry, ed. *Postmodern Fiction: A Bio-Bibliographical Guide*. Movements in the Arts 2. Westport, Ct.: Greenwood Press, 1986.

Provides basic primary and secondary checklists for a wide range of contemporary experimental writers whose work is not treated by other reference tools. For each author included, a record of books and uncollected periodical contributions precedes a selected, unannotated list of critical commentary on the writer. Prefacing this bibliographical information is an essay that reviews the author's work and its reception.

30. Nadel, Ira Bruce. *Jewish Writers of North America: A Guide to Information Sources*. American Studies Information Guide Series 8. Detroit: Gale, 1981.

    Includes a substantial section for Jewish-American novelists and short story writers, most of whom are contemporary figures. For each, it provides enumerative coverage of books, with separate lists for their fiction, nonfiction prose, screenplays, and other genres as appropriate; their contributions to periodicals are occasionally recorded, especially interviews with them. Secondary treatment is highly selective and lightly annotated.

31. Radcliffe, Elsa J. *Gothic Novels of the Twentieth Century: An Annotated Bibliography*. Metuchen, N.J.: Scarecrow Press, 1979.

    Consists of alphabetically arranged, single-author checklists of Gothic fiction published predominantly since the 1950s, by writers many of whom are American. Introduction explains the definition of Gothic fiction employed in this volume. Many entries carry annotations, which are informal and range from plot summaries to critical evaluation.

32. Reginald, R. *Contemporary Science Fiction Authors*. New York: Arno Press, 1974. Rpt. with corrections of *Stella Nova: The Contemporary Science Fiction Authors*. Los Angeles: Unicorn, 1970.

    Records enumerative, chronological coverage of the science fiction books of nearly 500 English-language writers who were practicing the genre during the period 1960-1968. No periodical or secondary sources indicated.

33. ----------. *Science Fiction and Fantasy Literature: A Checklist. 1700-1974*. 2 vols. Detroit: Gale, 1979.

    Vol. 1 is an alphabetically arranged author list that records English-language first editions of each writer's books. Includes

15

many contemporary Americans, some of whom are the subjects of little other bibliographic study.

34. Reilly, John M., ed. *Twentieth-Century Crime and Mystery Writers*. 2nd ed. New York: St. Martin's Press; London: St. James Press, 1985. 1st ed. 1980.

Reliably furnishes for each of more than 600 English-language writers, a basic, enumerative record of their books and a checklist of their uncollected fiction published in periodicals. Many of these authors are contemporary Americans, for whom no other bibliographic coverage is available. Occasional but extremely limited references to the secondary literature.

35. *Repertorio Bibliografico della Letterature Americana in Italia*. Ed. Biancamaria Tedeschini Lalli, Robert Perrault, and Alessandra Pinto Surdi. 4 vols. Rome: Edizioni di Storia e Letteratura, 1966-1982.

With each volume covering a five-year period, the set furnishes a twenty-year record of Italian editions of American writers and critical commentary on them from 1945-1964. Books as well as periodical articles and reviews are listed. Among contemporary writers of fiction included are William Burroughs, Truman Capote, William Goyen, Joseph Heller, Norman Mailer, Bernard Malamud, James Purdy, Philip Roth, J.D. Salinger, John Updike, and Gore Vidal.

36. Rosa, Alfred F., and Paul A. Eschholz. *Contemporary Fiction in America and England, 1950-1970, A Guide to Information Sources*. American Literature, English Literature, and World Literatures in English Information Guide Series 10. Detroit: Gale, 1976.

Provides enumerative primary and unannotated secondary coverage of eighty American novelists and short story writers whose first or major work was published between 1950 and 1970. Primary references limited to separately published books, while list of secondary sources excludes most reviews and concentrates on major critical pieces. Citations to 1970.

37. Rubin, Louis D., Jr., ed. *A Bibliographical Guide to the Study of Southern Literature*. Baton Rouge: Louisiana State Univ. Press, 1969.

A substantial portion of this volume is devoted to unannotated, single-author checklists of secondary studies. Numerous contemporary fiction writers are included, with the coverage particularly valuable for minor writers not otherwise the subject of bibliographical study.

38. Rush, Theresa Gunnels, Carol Fairbanks Myers, and Esther Spring Arata. *Black American Writers Past and Present: A Biographical and Bibliographical Dictionary*. 2 vols. Metuchen, N.J.: Scarecrow Press, 1975.

Provides primary and secondary checklists for a very broad range of Afro-American writers, most of whom began their publishing careers after 1945. Enumerative treatment of works by the writers is arranged according to genre and typically includes books and contributions to books as well as periodical pieces. Unannotated record of writings about an author separates biographical from critical references, extending to reviews, particularly when they constitute the only secondary source. Very useful for some less well known writers who are not within the scope of more general reference tools. Citations into 1974.

39. Schlobin, Roger C. *The Literature of Fantasy: A Comprehensive, Annotated Bibliography of Modern Fantasy Fiction*. Garland Reference Library of the Humanities 176. New York: Garland, 1979.

Focused on modern adult fantasy fiction, this reference tool provides checklists of books by a wide range of twentieth-century English-language writers, including numerous contemporary Americans. A plot description accompanies each entry for a novel; contents notes are furnished for short story collections. Except for bibliographies, secondary references are excluded, as are the individual writer's contributions to periodicals.

40. Smith, Curtis C., ed. *Twentieth-Century Science Fiction Writers*. 2nd ed. London and Chicago: St. James Press, 1986. 1st ed. 1981.

    Furnishes consistently reliable checklists of books and uncollected periodical publications by numerous contemporary American writers, along with a selective but quite useful record of major critical studies. Virtually all major and many minor practitioners of the science-fiction genre receive attention in the volume.

41. Smith, Myron J., Jr. *Cloak and Dagger: An Annotated Guide to Spy Thrillers*. 2nd ed. Santa Barbara, Calif.: ABC-Clio, 1982. 1st ed. 1975.

    Concentrating on English-language spy fiction written since World War II, this tool offers an alphabetically arranged author list of novels and story collections. For each title, basic bibliographical and plot summary information is supplied. Coverage reaches into early 1981.

42. *Starmont Reader's Guides to Contemporary Science Fiction and Fantasy Authors*. Series editor: Roger C. Schlobin. Originally published: Mercer Island, Wash.: Starmont House; Currently published: San Bernardino, Calif.: Borgo Press.

    Since its first volume appeared in 1979, this continuing series of pamphlet-length introductions to leading supernatural fiction writers has covered more than thirty prominent individuals. Each book concludes with selective primary and secondary bibliographies, whose entries often bear full annotations, summarizing both the plots of fictional items and the arguments of critical pieces. Treatment of an author's writings varies in depth among the volumes but usually includes periodical contributions as well as separate publications. Only the major secondary references are recorded in the lists of writings about an author. Volumes in the series are especially valuable for figures not otherwise the subject of extensive bibliographic analysis; they are also useful for updating older bibliographies.

43. Trujillo, Roberto G., and Andres Rodriguez. *Literatura Chicana: Creative and Critical Writings Through 1984*. Oakland, Calif.: Floricanto Press, 1985.

    Separate, alphabetically organized lists of Mexican-American novels and short stories include works by many contemporary writers in English. These sections as well as the volume's coverage of general Chicano literary criticism effectively extends and updates Items 15 and 28.

44. Tuck, Donald H. *The Encyclopedia of Science Fiction and Fantasy through 1968*. 3 vols. Chicago: Advent Publishers, 1974-1982.

    The first two volumes of this reference tool consist of brief biographies and densely packed bibliographies of science fiction writers and editors, many of whom are contemporary American figures. Enumerative entries for primary texts record variant editions as well as foreign-language translations and conclude with a brief plot summary. Treatment of collections specifies contents. Most valuable for its historical coverage, since citations cease with 1968; no secondary references.

45. *Twayne's United States Author Series*. Boston: G.K. Hall, 1961-.

    Many volumes in this monographic series of introductory studies of American writers are devoted to contemporary fiction writers. Each book concludes with a selective bibliography of primary and secondary references. Entries for the criticism on the writers are usually well annotated. Occasionally these checklists are substantial, constituting important additions to the author's bibliography; where this is the case, the volume has been individually treated in the Single Author section that follows.

46. Tymn, Marshall B., Roger C. Schlobin, and L.W. Currey. *A Research Guide to Science Fiction Studies: An Annotated Checklist of Primary and Secondary Sources for Fantasy and Science Fiction*. Garland Reference Library of the Humanities 87. New York: Garland, 1977.

    A comprehensive listing of the important reference sources published in the United States and England through 1976, this volume not only describes and evaluates the field's general bibliographic tools but also features a substantial section devoted to single-author studies, which usefully complements other compilations of secondary literature on individual writers.

47. Vinson, James, ed. *Contemporary Novelists*. 4th ed. London: St. James Press, 1986. 3rd ed. 1981; 2nd ed. 1976; 1st ed. 1972.

    Furnishes basic but very reliable primary and secondary bibliographical information for approximately 600 practicing English-language novelists, many of whom are American. Enumerative treatment of writings by each author concentrates on separately published works, listing items in all genres; uncollected fiction from periodicals is also noted. Highly selective, unannotated record of critical studies concludes the bibliographic account. Especially valuable in the case of newer writers for whom more extensive checklists are not yet available.

48. ----------, ed. *Twentieth-Century Romance and Gothic Writers*. London: Macmillan; Detroit: Gale, 1982.

    Offers enumerative checklists of the novels and other booklength publications of more than 300 writers of romance and Gothic fiction, including numerous contemporary American authors. Where secondary critical commentary is available, that is noted as well.

49. ----------, ed. *Twentieth-Century Western Writers*. London: Macmillan; Detroit: Gale, 1982.

This reference tool's wide scope extends to numerous contemporary writers of the American West, including not only novelists of strictly regional interest but also figures with national reputations, for example Edward Abbey, Thomas Berger, William Eastlake, Thomas McGuane, Larry McMurtry, Wallace Stegner, and Douglas Woolf. For each entry, provides a reliable record of the books and uncollected periodical contributions by the writer, along with a selected list of secondary references.

50. Walden, Daniel. *Twentieth-Century American-Jewish Fiction Writers*. Dictionary of Literary Biography 28. Detroit: Bruccoli Clark/Gale, 1984.

Offers basic primary and secondary checklists for more than fifty writers, many of whom are contemporary. Numerous figures treated have not yet been the subject of extensive bibliographical analysis, among them E.L. Doctorow, Irvin Faust, Bruce Jay Friedman, Erica Jong, Wallace Markfield, Jay Neugeboren, Susan Fromberg Schaeffer, and Jerome Weidman. Coverage of works by these writers emphasizes books, major uncollected periodical pieces, and interviews. Selected record of critical commentary for each is not annotated.

51. Walker, Warren S. *Twentieth-Century Short Story Explication: Interpretations 1900-1975, of Short Fiction since 1800*. 3rd ed. Hamden, Ct.: Shoe String Press, 1977. *Supplement I to Third Edition, 1975-1979, 1980; Supplement II to Third Edition, 1979-1981, 1984; Supplement III to Third Edition, 1981-1984, 1987*.

Organized alphabetically by author, then subarranged by story title, this multi-volume reference tool furnishes lists of secondary references to short fiction. Entries are drawn from books as well as periodicals and are predominantly English-language, though some Western European items appear. No annotations.

52. Weixlmann, Joe. *American Short-Fiction Criticism and Scholarship, 1959-1977: A Checklist*. Chicago: Swallow Press, 1982.

Complements Item 51, listing many citations to the secondary literature of short fiction published prior to 1978 but omitted from Walker's set. The alphabetical organization by individual writer is similar to Walker, but there is more emphasis on interviews with authors as well as on general and bibliographical studies.

53. Yancy, Preston M. *The Afro-American Short Story: A Comprehensive, Annotated Index with Selected Commentaries*. Bibliographies and Indexes in Afro-American and African Studies 10. Westport, Ct.: Greenwood Press, 1986.

Focuses on contemporary black American short stories published in anthologies, collections, and periodicals during the period 1950-1982. The volume's alphabetically arranged Author Index provides checklists of short fiction by individual writers, many of whom have not otherwise been bibliographically analyzed. Even for more prominent Afro-American writers who have been the subject of bibliographic work, the information furnished here may still be unique.

Single-Author Studies

ALBERT, MARVIN H. (1924-)

*54. Roger, Martin, compiler. Special issue of *Les Durs à cuire [Hard Boiled Dicks]* (1 November 1981).

> Item 2 reports that the forty-four page first number of this French journal devoted to American crime fiction contains a bibliography and filmography of Albert's work.

ALEXANDER, LLOYD (1924-)

55. Zahorski, Kenneth, and Robert H. Boyer. *Lloyd Alexander, Evangeline Walton Ensley, Kenneth Morris: A Primary and Secondary Bibliography*. Boston: G.K. Hall, 1981, esp. 3-110.

> Comprehensive coverage of English-language publications by and about Alexander through 1979. Chronologically organized primary coverage is divided into separate sections for fiction and nonfiction, with books treated enumeratively. Secondary account, which includes extensive references to reviews, is also arranged chronologically, with each entry thoroughly annotated.

ALGREN, NELSON (1909-1981)

56. McCollum, Kenneth G. *Nelson Algren: A Checklist*. Detroit: Bruccoli Clark/Gale, 1973.

Covers works by Algren into 1973. Highly abbreviated descriptions of books precede separate sections devoted to the original periodical appearances of stories, articles, reviews, and poems. Informal notes provide facts about the publication circumstances of periodical pieces but their subsequent incorporation into books is not noted. Except for facsimile reproductions and anecdotal material, fully superseded by Item 59.

57.   Studing, Richard. "A Nelson Algren Checklist." *Twentieth-Century Literature* 19.1 (January 1973): 27-39.

Registers writings both by and about Algren through 1970. The unannotated coverage of secondary materials is unique and includes reviews as well as more formal critical commentary.

58.   Garon, Paul. Algren in Paperback: A Checklist." *Paperback Quarterly* 5 (Winter 1982): 50-60.

Narrative accounts of the paperback publishing history of each of Algren's books precedes a tabular summary of printing data, including press runs. Foreign-language editions are excluded. Citations extend into 1977.

59.   Bruccoli, Matthew J. *Nelson Algren: A Descriptive Bibliography*. Pittsburgh: Univ. of Pittsburgh Press, 1985.

Exhaustive coverage of Algren's writings through 1984, including his reviews and book blurbs. Full descriptions of separately published items extend to book jackets and are supplemented by numerous photographic reproductions. Subsequent appearances of original periodical publications are also noted, along with indication of revision. Detailed indexes.

ALLEN, HENRY WILSON (1912-)

60.   Walker, Dale L. · "Henry Wilson Allen: A Chronological Bibliography," "An Allen Filmography," and "Works about

Allen." In *Will Henry's West*. El Paso: Texas Western Press, 1984, 203-208.

Bibliographical information fully superseded by Item 61, except for filmography.

61. Kroll, Keith. "Henry W. Allen (Will Henry/Clay Fisher): A Bibliography of Primary and Secondary Sources." *Bulletin of Bibliography* 44.4 (December 1987): 219-231.

Exemplary account through 1985 both of writings by Allen under his own name and various pseudonyms as well as about his work. Sections presenting primary materials are arranged chronologically: the enumerative record of books scrupulously lists variant editions, including foreign-language translations, while the detailed inventories of short stories and nonfiction contributed to periodicals also note reprintings and translations. The unannotated secondary section concentrates on critical and biographical pieces, excluding reviews.

ANAYA, RUDOLFO A. (1937-)

62. Marquez, Teresa. "Works by and about Rudolfo A. Anaya." In *The Magic of Words: Rudolfo A. Anaya and His Writings*. Ed. Paul Vassallo. Albuquerque: Univ. of New Mexico Press, 1982, 55-81.

Lists in a single alphabet primary and secondary materials through 1981. Annotations accompany all entries: the plots and themes of Anaya's fiction are briefly summarized, while the arguments of critical pieces, including reviews, are summarized. Range of reference is wide, including many citations to small press publications and local newspaper sources.

ANDERSON, POUL (1926-)

*63. Peyton, Roger D. *A Checklist of Poul Anderson*. Birmingham, Eng.: Privately printed, 1965.

Described by Robert E. Briney and Edward Wood in *SF Bibliographies: An Annotated Bibliography of Bibliographical Works on Science Fiction and Fantasy Fiction* (Chicago: Advent Publishers, 1972) as a generally complete checklist of Anderson's science fiction and fantasy writings into 1965, excluding his mysteries, historical fiction, and nonfiction.

64. "Poul Anderson Bibliography." *Magazine of Fantasy and Science Fiction* 40.4 (April 1971): 56-63.

Chronological coverage of primary materials, divided into sections for Anderson's novels, his collections, his edited books, his articles, essays, and reviews, his verse, and finally the short stories. Emphasis is on original appearances, excluding reprints, anthologizations, and translations but noting title changes. References extend into 1971. Also reports the existence of a more detailed bibliography by Mark Owings in *Washington Science Fiction Association Journal* 69 (1970), a copy of which was not, however, seen.

65. Benson, Gordon, Jr. *Poul Anderson: Myth-Master and Wonder-Weaver: An Interim Bibliography (1947-1986)*. 4th ed. Albuquerque: Galactic Central, 1987. 1st ed. 1982.

Fourth edition provides detailed account of Anderson's short stories, poems, and books into 1986. Alphabetical list of his contributions to periodicals carefully records reprintings in other magazines as well as in anthologies and Anderson's own collections. Enumerative, alphabetical coverage of books also fully registers subsequent reprintings and new editions. No foreign-language references or secondary citations.

ANGELOU, MAYA (1928-)

66. Cameron, Dee Birch. "A Maya Angelou Bibliography." *Bulletin of Bibliography* 36.1 (January-March 1979): 50-52.

Thorough coverage of works by and about Angelou into 1977. Enumerative checklist of primary sources includes unpublished plays; secondary treatment incorporates both reviews and articles but is not annotated.

ARD, WILLIAM (1922-1960)

67. Nevins, Francis M., Jr. "The World of William Ard." *Armchair Detective* 15.2 (1982): 158-166.

Enumerative checklist of Ard's novels published under his own name and several pseudonyms. Arranged chronologically under appropriate name or pseudonym with references to 1962.

ASIMOV, ISAAC (1920-)

68. A[simov], I[saac]. "Isaac Asimov: A Bibliography." *Magazine of Fantasy and Science Fiction* 31.4 (October 1966): 36-45.

Selective but extensive checklist of primary sources, including books and periodical appearances, into 1966; excludes anthologies, foreign publications, and shorter nonfiction pieces, introductions, and letters to the editor.

69. Miller, Marjorie M. *Isaac Asimov: A Checklist of Works Published in the United States, March 1939-May 1972*. Serif Series 25. Kent, Ohio: Kent State Univ. Press, 1972.

Deliberately restricted account of works by and about Asimov into 1972. Enumerative checklist of Asimov's separate and periodical publications is arranged chronologically and records many reprintings of items. Except for British and Canadian editions of books, primary coverage is limited to American materials. Highly selective secondary section excludes reviews but accompanies each entry with contents notes.

70. Cox, David M., and Gary R. Libby. "A Bibliography of Major Science Fiction Works through 1976." In *Isaac Asimov*. Ed. Joseph D. Olander and Martin Harry Greenberg. New York: Taplinger, 1977, 217-233.

Enumerative coverage of Asimov's science fiction writings, deliberately excluding all other types of publications. Abbreviated entries are arranged alphabetically. Draws on Item 69, updating Miller's coverage by several years.

AUCHINCLOSS, LOUIS (1917-)

71. Bryer, Jackson R. *Louis Auchincloss and His Critics: A Bibliographical Record*. Boston: G.K. Hall, 1977.

Lists works by and about Auchincloss into 1976. Primary coverage is enumerative and limited to principal English-language editions but does extend to published legal notes and letters to the editor. Annotated treatment of secondary materials is more thorough and includes summaries of most American and British reviews. Sound index.

AVALLONE, MICHAEL (1924-)

72. Mertz, Stephen. "Michael Avallone: A Checklist." *Armchair Detective* 9.2 (February 1976): 132-134.

Enumerative checklist of Avallone's novels, along with their film and television adaptations, with references into 1975. Organization is by byline, beginning with Avallone and continuing through his numerous pseudonyms.

*73. "Michael Avallone." *Amis du crime* 8 (February 1981).

Item 2 reports that this issue of the French crime magazine is devoted to Avallone and contains a bibliography of American and French editions of his books, along with a checklist of his short stories.

BALDWIN, JAMES (1924-1987)

74. Kindt, Kathleen A. "James Baldwin: A Checklist, 1947-1962." *Bulletin of Bibliography* 24.6 (January-April 1965): 123-126.

Enumerative record of Baldwin's works arranged alphabetically by title within their different genres; unannotated list of reviews and criticism of his books also arranged alphabetically by author.

75. Fischer, Russell G. "James Baldwin: A Bibliography, 1947-1962." *Bulletin of Bibliography* 24.6 (January-April 1965): 127-130.

Essentially duplicates both the structure and scope of Item 74 but does register some different items; also, coverage of reviews structured by titles of Baldwin's books, rather than the piece's author.

76. Standley, Fred L. "James Baldwin: A Checklist, 1963-1967." *Bulletin of Bibliography* 25.6 (May-August 1968): 135-137, 160.

Supplements and updates coverage of primary and secondary materials provided by Items 74 and 75. Entries unannotated.

*77. Jones, Mary E. *James Baldwin*. CAAS Bibliography 5. Atlanta: Atlanta University, Center for African and African American Studies, n.d. [c.1970].

Dance in Item 80 reports that incomplete, omitted, or erroneous data sometimes mar this checklist but that it remains valuable for its listing of unpublished Baldwin manuscripts in the Atlanta University Library.

78. O'Daniel, Therman B. "James Baldwin: A Classified Bibliography." In *James Baldwin: A Critical Evaluation*. Washington, D.C.: Howard Univ. Press, 1977, 243-261.

Generically arranged checklist that records both primary and secondary items. Enumerative coverage of works by Baldwin is organized chronologically; unannotated record of writings about him is alphabetically presented.

79. Mauro, Walter. "Nota bibliografica." In *Baldwin*. Il Castoro 119. Firenze: La Nuova Italia, 1976, 149-152.

Especially valuable for its enumerative record of Italian translations of Baldwin's books as well as its unannotated list of Italian
reviews and other commentary on Baldwin by Italian critics.
Coverage into 1973.

80. Dance, Daryl. "James Baldwin." In *Black American Writers: Biblio-
     graphical Essays*. Vol. 2. Ed. M. Thomas Inge, Maurice Duke,
     and Jackson R. Bryer. New York: St. Martin's Press, 1978, 73-
     120.

     A selective but especially useful narrative survey of primary and
     secondary materials into 1976. The account of writings by
     Baldwin evaluates editions, summarizes interviews, and
     provides a census of manuscript sources. Discussion of com-
     mentary about Baldwin proceeds work by work, concluding
     with an indication of directions for new research.

81. Standley, Fred L., and Nancy V. Standley. *James Baldwin: A
     Reference Guide*. Boston: G.K. Hall, 1980.

     Brief enumerative lists of Baldwin's books and periodical con-
     tributions preface thorough chronological coverage of reviews
     and critical commentary. Detailed annotations for all secon-
     dary entries, and sound index by personal name, title, and sub-
     ject. Emphasis is on English-language materials, though some
     foreign-language sources are entered.

BARTH, JOHN (1930-)

82. Bryer, Jackson R. "Two Bibliographies." *Critique* 6.2 (Fall 1963):
     86-94, esp. 86-89.

     Lists works by Barth and records representative articles and
     reviews about him; coverage extends into 1963.

83. Weixlmann, Joseph N. "John Barth: A Bibliography." *Critique* 13.3
     (1972): 45-55.

Unannotated checklist of writings by and about Barth into 1971. List of secondary commentary excludes reviews. Completely superseded by Item 84.

84. ----------. *John Barth: A Descriptive Primary and Annotated Secondary Bibliography, Including a Descriptive Catalog of Manuscript Holdings in United States Libraries.* Garland Reference Library of the Humanities 25. New York: Garland, 1976.

Thorough record of writings both by and about Barth into 1975, including physical descriptions of manuscripts in American repositories. Formal bibliographic descriptions of both separate publications and contributions to books. Treatment of periodical pieces notes later publication in books. Coverage of secondary materials is arranged in sections for biographical commentary, criticism, and reviews, which are informatively annotated except for the last. Detailed indexes.

85. Vine, Richard Allan. *John Barth: An Annotated Bibliography.* Scarecrow Author Bibliographies 31. Metuchen, N.J.: Scarecrow Press, 1977.

Includes published work by and about Barth into 1975. Enumerative checklist of primary sources precedes thoroughly annotated record of reviews of Barth's books and of critical articles about him. This secondary coverage is extensive but deliberately not exhaustive.

86. Walsh, Thomas P., and Cameron Northouse. *John Barth, Jerzy Kosinski, and Thomas Pynchon: A Reference Guide.* Boston: G.K. Hall, 1977.

Chronological record of published works by and about Barth through 1973. Focus is on major items, both in the enumerative primary list and the annotated secondary section. Coverage not as detailed as in Items 84 and 85 but the chronological organization of critical commentary and the extensive annotations remain valuable.

BARTHELME, DONALD (1931-)

87. McCaffery, Larry. "Donald Barthelme, Robert Coover, William H. Gass: Three Checklists." *Bulletin of Bibliography* 31.3 (July-September 1974): 101-106, esp. 101-102, 106.

    Alphabetically arranged enumeration of Barthelme's published writings into 1972 (excluding early materials from Houston), followed by unannotated listing of secondary references. Fully superseded by Item 89.

88. Klinkowitz, Jerome. "Donald Barthelme: A Checklist, 1957-1974." *Critique* 16.3 (1975): 49-58.

    Exacting record of primary and secondary publications from Barthelme's first signed work in 1957 through 1974. Fully superseded by Item 89, except for the checklist's arrangement, which simplifies reconstruction of the original periodical appearances in short story collections.

89. Klinkowitz, Jerome, Asa Pieratt, and Robert Murray Davis. *Donald Barthelme: A Comprehensive Bibliography and Annotated Secondary Checklist.* Hamden, Ct.: Shoe String Press, 1977.

    Exhaustive record of materials both by and about Barthelme through 1976. Coverage of primary texts provides detailed physical descriptions of books and their variant English and foreign-language editions; it also includes a special section on Barthelme's early writings in Houston. While critical articles are annotated, reviews of Barthelme's works are listed without summaries.

90. Vitanza, Victor J. "Addendum to Klinkowitz: Donald Barthelme." *Papers of the Bibliographical Society of America* 73.3 (July-September 1979): 364.

    Records the 1967 publication of a short story in a local University of Houston magazine that was omitted from Item 89.

91. McCaffery, Larry. "Donald Barthelme (b.1931)." In *The Metafictional Muse: The Works of Robert Coover, Donald Barthelme, and William H. Gass*. Pittsburgh: Univ. of Pittsburgh Press, 1982, 287-290.

    Continues enumerative, unannotated style of Item 87 into 1982, though reviews of Barthelme's books are excluded.

BEATTIE, ANN (1947-)

92. Porter, Carolyn. "A Bibliography of Writings by Ann Beattie." In *Contemporary American Women Writers: Narrative Strategies*. Ed. Catherine Rainwater and William J. Scheick. Lexington: Univ. Press of Kentucky, 1985, 26-28.

    Useful checklist of Beattie's published writings into 1985. The chronological record of short stories she first published in periodicals notes subsequent printings in Beattie's own collections as well as in composite anthologies.

93. Opperman, Harry, and Christina Murphy. "Ann Beattie (1947-): A Checklist." *Bulletin of Bibliography* 44.2 (June 1987): 111-118.

    Thorough presentation of writings by and about Beattie through 1986 and into early 1987. Primary coverage is arranged chronologically within types of publication: the enumerative record of books notes variant editions, and the treatment of periodical contributions carefully identifies reprintings. Unannotated secondary coverage includes separate sections for interviews, articles, and reviews.

BEAUMONT, CHARLES (1929-1967)

94. Nolan, William F. "A Charles Beaumont Index: 1951-1965." *Magazine of Fantasy and Science Fiction* 32.6 (June 1967): 71-72.

Enumerative treatment of books and brief account of uncollected stories through 1965. Completely superseded by Nolan's later work.

95. ----------. "Charles Beaumont: A Bibliographical Note and a Checklist." *Armchair Detective* 18.1 (Winter 1985): 41-46.

Scrupulously thorough account of Beaumont's work throughout his life, with additional notice of posthumous collections and reprintings into 1984. Both his science fiction and detective-suspense writings are covered, as well as his screenplays, teleplays, and nonfiction periodical contributions. Treatment of short stories in magazines records subsequent republication and also notes Beaumont's collaboration whenever relevant. Secondary references are excluded.

96. ----------. *The Work of Charles Beaumont: An Annotated Bibliography and Guide*. Bibliographies of Modern Authors 6. San Bernardino, Calif.: Borgo Press, 1986.

Refines and elaborates the format of Item 95, expanding coverage into 1986. The chronological record of Beaumont's work is arranged in sections according to its various media and includes enumerative treatment of his books, supplemented by detailed notes on their contents, a thorough listing of the reprintings of his stories, and separate accounts of his nonfiction articles, screenplays, and television scripts. Lightly annotated checklist of secondary references concludes the work.

BECKHAM, BARRY (1944-)

97. Weixlmann, Joe. "Barry Beckham: A Bibliography." *College Language Association Journal* 24.4 (June 1981): 522-528.

Exacting record of writings by and about Beckham into 1981. Enumerative primary coverage thoroughly notes variant editions of the novels as well as his contributions to many black American journals. Secondary treatment is equally detailed, including numerous references to local newspapers and other unindexed sources.

BELLOW, SAUL (1915-)

98. Schneider, Harold W. "Two Bibliographies: Saul Bellow, William Styron." *Critique* 3.3 (Summer 1960): 71-91, esp. 72-86.

    Checklist of published materials by and about Bellow. Most reviews and all critical/biographical entries receive generous annotations.

99. Sokoloff, B.A., and Mark E. Posner. *Saul Bellow: A Comprehensive Bibliography*. Folcroft, Pa.: Folcroft Press, 1971.

    Enumerative, chronological account of published writings by Bellow and unannotated, alphabetical checklist of commentary about him, through 1968. Fully superseded by later book-length bibliographies.

100. Lercangée, Francine. *Saul Bellow: A Bibliography of Secondary Sources*. Brussels: Center for American Studies, 1977.

    Unannotated record of published articles and reviews about Bellow to mid-1977. International in scope, the checklist is arranged alphabetically within a scheme classified principally by individual novel. Coverage of European references not fully superseded.

101. Nault, Marianne. *Saul Bellow: His World and His Critics: An Annotated International Bibliography*. Garland Reference Library of the Humanities 59. New York: Garland, 1977.

    In-depth treatment of materials by and about Bellow into 1976. Primary sections include enumerative lists of separate publications and their translations, annotated record of periodical contributions, and detailed accounts of manuscript holdings at the Universities of Chicago and Texas-Austin. Secondary coverage features an abbreviated selection of reviews and an alphabetically arranged record of criticism with generous contents notes. Remains valuable for its census of unpublished archival sources; otherwise, largely superseded by Item 105.

102. Noreen, Robert G. *Saul Bellow: A Reference Guide*. Boston: G.K. Hall, 1978.

Sound chronological record of secondary commentary, including representative foreign language materials, through 1976. Though its bibliographical coverage has been essentially superseded by Item 105, annotations remain valuable, both supplementing and complementing the contents notes by Cronin and Hall.

103. Field, Leslie, and John Z. Guzlowski. "Criticism of Saul Bellow: A Selected Checklist." *Modern Fiction Studies* 25.1 (Spring 1979): 149-171.

Conveniently organized by category of critical commentary, this unannotated record of secondary sources has separate sections for general criticism, interviews, and short stories as well as for each of Bellow's books. Bibliographic information fully incorporated in Item 105.

104. Cronin, Gloria L. "Saul Bellow: Selected and Annotated Bibliography." *Saul Bellow Journal* 4.1-6.2 (Fall-Winter 1985-Winter 1987).

Each of these six issues contains a highly selective but thoroughly annotated checklist of criticism that appeared annually from 1980 through 1985; subsequent numbers of the journal promise to continue this practice, thus prospectively serving to update the coverage Cronin and Hall provide in Item 105.

105. Cronin, Gloria L., and Blaine H. Hall. *Saul Bellow: An Annotated Bibliography*. 2nd ed. Garland Reference Library of the Humanities 679. New York: Garland, 1987.

Enumerative primary and annotated secondary record through 1985 and into 1986. Coverage of Bellow's published work omits some early short publications that appeared later in revised versions; otherwise quite exhaustive, including careful lists of foreign-language translations and reprintings of periodical pieces. Classified treatment of criticism is arranged predominantly by individual novel; items included in this virtually comprehensive list of commentary are fully annotated, except for insubstantial reviews and doctoral dissertations. Some brief notices have been deliberately excluded.

BERGER, THOMAS (1924-)

106. Bense, James. "Works by and about Thomas Berger." *Studies in American Humor* ns 2.2 (Fall 1983): 142-152.

Thorough enumerative treatment of works by Berger and selective, unannotated coverage of commentary about him, into 1983. Primary references are arranged chronologically within type of publication, including sections for Berger's nonfiction articles and critical reviews. Secondary record is comprehensive for extended discussions of Berger but excludes minor reviews of his novels.

BERRY, WENDELL (1934-)

107. Lalka, David G. *Wendell Berry: A Descriptive Checklist*. Macomb, Ill.: Privately printed, 1972.

Briefly descriptive treatment of published books by Berry and unannotated list of items about him, with references through 1971.

108. Hicks, Jack. "A Wendell Berry Checklist." *Bulletin of Bibliography* 37.3 (July-September 1980): 127-131.

Coverage through April 1978 of writings by and about Berry. Primary sources are arranged chronologically within genre and type of publication. The enumerative lists of novels and books of poetry duly note their variant editions; the separate records of Berry's uncollected prose and poetry include numerous citations to nonliterary journals. Unannotated secondary section is divided between reviews and articles, with frequent references to local newspapers and regional publications.

BISHOP, MICHAEL (1945-)

109.   Nee, Dave. *Michael Bishop: A Preliminary Bibliography*. Berkeley, Calif.: Other Change of Hobbit, 1983.

Highly informative account of Bishop's writings into mid-1983, with separate, alphabetically arranged sections for his books and edited anthologies as well as for the fiction, nonfiction, poetry, and book reviews first published in periodicals. Treatment of books is enumerative but records variant editions, indicating also original price and cover artist. Handling of magazine pieces consistently notes reprintings. Chronological and title indexes provide alternate approaches to the bibliography's dominantly alphabetical organization. No secondary citations.

BLISH, JAMES (1921-1975)

110.   Owings, Mark. "James Blish: Bibliography." *Magazine of Fantasy and Science Fiction* 42.4 (April 1972): 78-83.

Furnishes enumerative, alphabetically arranged coverage of Blish's fictional writings through 1971. Variant editions of books are recorded, including translations into foreign languages. Entries for stories register only original appearances, except for serialization of work later published in book form and stories expanded into novels. Blish's criticism and his editorial work are briefly noted in a separate section.

*111. Blish, Judith A. *James Blish: A Bibliography 1940-1976*. Privately printed, 1976.

Not seen; recorded in Item 10.

BLOCH, ROBERT (1917-)

112. Hall, Graham M. *Robert Bloch Bibliography.* Tewkesbury, Gloucestershire, Eng.: Graham M. Hall, 1965.

Two-part checklist of Bloch's published fiction and nonfiction through late 1964. The first section chronologically enumerates works, including reprints and foreign-language translations. The second part covers magazine fiction, arranged alphabetically by periodical title. A highly condensed addendum lists anthology and other miscellaneous book appearances, contents of short story collections, and information about his work in radio, film, and television.

*113. Larson, Randall D., ed. *The Robert Bloch Fanzine.* Los Altos, Calif.: Fandom Unlimited Enterprises, 1972. 2nd ed. 1973.

Item 2 describes the bibliography included in this volume as an expansion of Item 112, presenting Bloch's magazine fiction, nonfiction, books, columns, and interviews--including pseudonymous pieces, reprints, and translations--in a single chronological list, supplemented by information on his contributions to radio, television, and films.

*114. "Bibliographie" for "Dossier Robert Bloch." *Polar* 3 (June 1979): 30-35.

Cited in Item 2 and remarked for its inclusion of comments on his fiction by Bloch himself. The journal is published in France.

115. Flanagan, Graeme. *Robert Bloch: A Bio-Bibliography.* Canberra: By the Author, 1979.

Intended to provide comprehensive coverage of Bloch's work into 1979, the checklist is divided into a number of sections: American and British editions of the novels and story collections, first appearances of stories and of nonfiction pieces in magazines, and miscellaneous items such as interviews and speeches. This bibliographical information is supplemented by an account of Bloch's work in radio, television, and films.

*116. Bloch, Robert N. *Robert Bloch: Eine Deutsche Bibliographie.* Giessen, W. Germany: Munniksma, 1986.

Reported by Larson in Item 117 to cover West German and Scandinavian publications; the compiler is not related to Bloch.

117. Larson, Randall D. *The Complete Robert Bloch: An Illustrated, International Bibliography.* Sunnyvale, Calif.: Fandom Unlimited Enterprises, 1986; San Bernardino, Calif.: Borgo Press, 1987.

An impressively thorough account of Bloch's work into 1987, compiled with the writer's active cooperation. Alphabetically arranged sections for short stories, novels, short story collections, nonfiction, introductions, radio, television, and film adaptations, interviews, and Bloch's numerous contributions to fanzines--supplemented by indexes for magazines cited and subjects. Treatment of books is enumerative but records variant editions, including detailed listing of translations; handling of short stories first published in periodicals carefully inventories subsequent printings in anthologies as well as in other magazines, including foreign-language journals. Illustrated by photographic reproductions of the covers of books and magazines.

BOURJAILY, VANCE (1922-)

118. McMillan, William, and John M. Muste. "A Vance Bourjaily Checklist." *Critique* 17.3 (1976): 105-110.

Extensive record of writings by and about Bourjaily into 1975. Enumerative coverage of primary materials notes variant editions and also provides information on the publishing history of periodical pieces. Unannotated lists of reviews and other criticism concentrate on national publications, without noting local newspaper responses to the novels.

BOWLES, PAUL (1911-)

119. McLeod, Cecil R. *Paul Bowles: A Checklist*. [Flint, Mich.]: Apple Tree Press, 1970.

Reliable enumerative record of primary printed materials, divided by type of work. Variant editions of books and publishing history of individual periodical pieces noted. Superseded by Item 120.

120. Miller, Jeffrey. *Paul Bowles: A Descriptive Bibliography*. Santa Barbara, Calif.: Black Sparrow Press, 1986.

Model descriptive treatment of Bowles's work, arranged chronologically within type of material. Includes not only his books, translations, and published music but also unpublished music, phonodiscs, and miscellaneous items. Very detailed indexing.

BRACKETT, LEIGH (1915-1978)

121. Arbur, Rosemarie. *Leigh Brackett, Marion Zimmer Bradley, Anne McCaffrey: A Primary and Secondary Bibliography*. Boston: G.K. Hall, 1982.

Thorough checklist of published writings by and about Brackett into early 1980. The enumerative primary coverage is arranged chronologically within the categories of fiction, miscellaneous media (especially, screenplays and teleplays) and nonfiction (with contents notes); scope is exhaustive, though some fanzine contributions may be missing. Well annotated secondary section is more selective, focusing on critical commentary devoted to Brackett's science fiction.

BRADBURY, RAY (1920-)

122. Nolan, William F. "The Ray Bradbury Index." In *Ray Bradbury Review*. Ed. William F. Nolan. San Diego, Calif.: William F. Nolan, 1952, 46-63.

Primary coverage of Bradbury's fiction and nonfiction as well as reprints, anthologizations, and radio and television adaptations, through 1951. Essentially superseded by Item 125.

123. ----------. "An Index to the Works of Ray Bradbury." *Magazine of Fantasy and Science Fiction* 24.5 (May 1963): 40-51.

Record of Bradbury's works through 1962 arranged chronologically within type of publication, with separate sections for books, stories, poems, screen and radio scripts, book introductions, and nonfiction. Primary coverage followed by brief list of material on Bradbury. Bibliographic information incorporated in Item 125.

124. ----------. "The Published Books and Stories of Ray Bradbury." In Ray Bradbury, *Martian Chronicles*. Garden City, N.Y.: Doubleday, 1973, 276-298.

Detailed chronological record of Bradbury's published fiction through 1972. Essentially superseded by Item 125.

125. ----------. *The Ray Bradbury Companion: A Life and Career History, Photolog, and Comprehensive Checklist of Writings with Facsimiles from Ray Bradbury's Unpublished and Uncollected Work in All Media*. Detroit: Bruccoli Clark/Gale, 1975.

An informal record that neglects many bibliographical conventions but nonetheless provides a very informative account of materials both by and about Bradbury through 1973. Based on the compiler's personal collection, the checklist is arranged generically and records the full range of Bradbury's contributions to popular culture, including his screenplays, radio scripts, contributions to privately published fanzines, and teleplays as well as the better known novels and short stories. Coverage of secondary sources, especially reviews, is highly selective.

126. Allbright, Donn. "Ray Bradbury Index." *Xenophile* 13 (May 1975): 10-20, 61-66; 26 (September 1976): 4-10; 36 (November 1977): 2-7.

> Designated as supplemental indexes to Item 125, these articles make corrections to Nolan's *Companion*, note its omissions, and supplement it with more recently published items. Especially strong in references to fanzines and pulp magazines.

127. Nolan, William F. "Bradbury in the Pulps." *Xenophile* 36 (November 1977): R21-R24, R31.

> Provides a checklist of the fiction Bradbury contributed to pulp magazines from 1941-1950, accompanied by a supplementary index for more recent, unreprinted contributions. The stories are arranged chronologically under headings for the magazines in which they originally appeared; pieces that were never collected or anthologized are also indicated. Bibliographic information was essentially derived from Item 125, but the organization here is different and additional publishing data is furnished.

128. ----------. "Bradbury's First Book Appearances." *Xenophile* 36 (November 1977): R8-R12.

> A checklist of first book appearances, excluding pieces first published in booklets, pamphlets, and in Bradbury's own collections; foreign-language items are also omitted. Arrangement is chronological within genre, with separate sections for fiction, verse, and nonfiction. Significantly expands the coverage of first book appearances provided by Item 125.

129. ----------. "Bradbury's Textbook Appearances 1955-1972." *Xenophile* 36 (November 1977): R28-R29, R31.

> An informal checklist of Bradbury's stories subsequently printed in textbooks through 1972. Organized alphabetically by individual story, then chronologically, with editors and publishers of the textbooks omitted. This material had been

dropped from Item 125, so that its publication here significantly broadens the bibliographic account of Bradbury's popularity on the scholastic market.

130. Tymn, Marshall B. "Ray Bradbury: A Bibliography." In *Ray Bradbury*. Ed. Martin Harry Greenberg and Joseph D. Olander. New York: Taplinger, 1980, 227-241.

Checklist of works by and about Bradbury with references into 1978. Enumerative primary coverage is arranged alphabetically within genres of Bradbury's published writings; unannotated secondary treatment is selective, excluding reviews entirely. Useful for updating Item 125.

BRADLEY, MARION ZIMMER (1930-)

131. Arbur, Rosemarie. *Leigh Brackett, Marion Zimmer Bradley, Anne McCaffrey: A Primary and Secondary Bibliography*. Boston: G.K. Hall, 1982.

Sound primary and secondary record of publications into early 1980. Near exhaustive enumerative coverage of Bradley's fiction and nonfiction, the latter supplied with content notes. Entries for criticism concentrate on responses to Bradley's science fiction and are thoroughly annotated.

BRAUTIGAN, RICHARD (1933-1984)

132. Wanless, James, and Christine Kolodziej. "Richard Brautigan: A Working Checklist." *Critique* 16.1 (1974): 41-52.

Useful but flawed attempt to cover writings by and about Brautigan through 1973. Enumerative primary sections register variant editions of separate publications, record periodical contributions and their subsequent reprintings, and informally supply much interesting publishing history. Secondary section briefly annotates entries. The compilers acknowledge their inability to confirm numerous items.

133. Jones, Stephen R. "Richard Brautigan: A Bibliography." *Bulletin of Bibliography* 33.1 (January 1976): 53-59.

> Chronological listings of works by Brautigan and alphabetical record of reviews and criticism about him through late 1975. Incorporates information from Item 132 and generally supersedes its coverage, except for Wanless and Kolodziej's miscellaneous notes on publishing history and their unorthodox but still useful arrangement.

BROWN, DEE (1908-)

134. Hagen, Lyman B. "Dee Alexander Brown." *Bulletin of Bibliography* 43.3 (September 1986): 172-178.

> Chronologically organized, enumerative checklist of Brown's fiction and nonfiction writings into 1983, followed by unannotated record of reviews and other secondary commentary. Primary coverage treats variant editions and translations of books as well as reprintings of periodical pieces.

BROWN, FREDRIC (1906-1972)

135. Baird, Newton. "A Fredric Brown Checklist: Paradox and Plot, Part V." *Armchair Detective* 10.4 (October 1977): 370-375; "A Fredric Brown Checklist: Paradox and Plot, Part VI." *Armchair Detective* 11.1 (January 1978): 86-91, 102.

> Highly detailed coverage of writings by and about Brown into 1977. Enumerative treatment of Brown's books encompasses both his detective and science fiction, records variant editions and translations, and provides a plot summary for each entry, followed by a list of reviews. Handling of short stories is similarly exacting, with notation of subsequent republication and changed titles. Unannotated list of critical commentary other than reviews constitutes the bibliography's final section.

*136. Schleret, Jean-Jacques. "Fredric Brown 1906-1972." *Les Amis du crime* 3 (c.1979).

Items 2 and 137 report this issue of the French crime fiction magazine is devoted to Brown and that it includes an excellent bibliography with sections for the French and American editions of the books, the short stories, collections, films and television adaptations, and secondary studies.

137. Baird, Newton. *A Key to Fredric Brown's Wonderland: A Study and an Annotated Bibliographical Checklist.* Georgetown, Calif.: Talisman Literary Research, 1981, esp. 27-53.

A revision and expansion of Item 135. Primary coverage is presented chronologically by genre and publication format, with an enumerative listing and annotation of all Brown's books, including reprint editions and foreign-language translations; a detailed account of the short stories and their republication; and a thorough inventory of television and film adaptations. Entries in the alphabetically arranged secondary sections are lightly annotated. Citations into 1980.

138. Naudon, Jean-François. "Bibliographie de Fredric Brown." *Polar* 23 (15 April 1982): 41-63.

Based on Items 136 and 137, this checklist chronologically enumerates Brown's novels and story collections, noting variant editions and translations, with special emphasis on French-language materials. This emphasis on French imprints continues in Naudon's alphabetical coverage of short stories Brown first published in periodicals. Complements previous bibliographic treatments and includes numerous reproductions of book jackets and wrappers.

139. Schleret, Jean-Jacques, and Newton Baird. "Filmographie de Fredric Brown." *Polar* 23 (15 April 1982): 64-68.

Covers adaptations of Brown's work for both film and television.

BRYANT, EDWARD (1945-)

*140. *Edward Bryant Bibliography*. Los Angeles: Swigart, 1980.

Recorded by Item 40. Not seen.

BUDRYS, ALGIS (1931-)

141. Drumm, Chris. *An Algis Budrys Checklist*. Polk City, Iowa: Chris Drumm, 1982. Rev. ed. in preparation, San Bernardino, Calif.: Borgo Press.

Detailed chronological account of Budrys' works into 1982. Enumerative treatment of books registers first as well as subsequent editions, recording total paginations and original publication prices for each. Coverage of stories and other contributions to periodicals includes reprintings in Budrys's own collections and in multi-author anthologies. No references to secondary literature.

BUKOWSKI, CHARLES (1920-)

142. Dorbin, Sanford. *A Bibliography of Charles Bukowski*. Los Angeles: Black Sparrow Press, 1969.

Comprehensively covers works by and about Bukowski into 1969. Fully describes separate publications, even ephemerae, with supplementary notes furnishing additional bibliographical information, including notation of different printings. Secondary section is lightly annotated.

143. Fox, Hugh. *Charles Bukowski: A Critical and Bibliographical Study*. Somerville, Mass.: Abyss Publications, 1969, esp. 96-121.

Limited to periodical appearances of Bukowski's work. Not as thorough as Item 142 but occasionally includes publications omitted by Dorbin.

BURROUGHS, WILLIAM S. (1914-)

144. Rushing, Lynda Lee. "William S. Burroughs: A Bibliography." *Bulletin of Bibliography* 29.3 (July-September 1972): 87-92.

   Enumerative checklist of works by Burroughs, including unusual miscellaneous items, accompanied by unannotated record of commentary and reviews about him, into 1971. Essentially superseded by the later book-length bibliographies listed below.

145. Skerl, Jennie. "A William S. Burroughs Bibliography." *Serif* 11.2 (Summer 1974): 12-20.

   Chronological list of materials by Burroughs and alphabetical record of writings about him into 1973. Enumerative treatment of books and other separately issued items is supplemented with brief notes about publishing history. Sound coverage of secondary sources includes many foreign-language pieces, though reviews are limited to British and American sources. Primary section superseded by Item 147; secondary listings complement Item 146.

146. Goodman, Michael B. *William S. Burroughs: An Annotated Bibliography of His Works and Criticism*. Garland Reference Library of the Humanities 24. New York: Garland, 1975.

   A heterogeneous record that treats both primary and secondary sources into 1975. Enumerative coverage of Burroughs's published texts is divided into separate, alphabetically arranged sections for his books, periodical contributions, and interviews; all these primary items are supplemented with useful contents notes. Similar descriptions are provided for the files of Burroughs's unpublished materials located in the archives of the Columbia University and Syracuse University Libraries. Reviews listed without annotation, but other secondary references are fully summarized.

147. Maynard, Joe, and Barry Miles. *William S. Burroughs: A Bibliography, 1953-1973*. Charlottesville: Univ. Press of Virginia, 1978.

Exhaustive account of Burroughs' published work through 1973, including interviews, foreign editions, obscure miscellaneous items, and recordings. Treatment of separate works is fully descriptive. List of periodical publications scrupulously notes reprintings. All sections arranged chronologically.

BUTLER, OCTAVIA E. (1947-)

148. Weixlmann, Joe. "An Octavia E. Butler Bibliography." *Black American Literature Forum* 18.2 (Summer 1984): 88-89.

Thorough record of writings by and about Butler into 1984. Enumerative primary coverage includes foreign-language translations of the novels as well as interviews appearing in science fiction and black American magazines. Checklist of criticism and reviews is similarly detailed, though not annotated.

CALISHER, HORTENSE (1911-)

149. Snodgrass, Kathleen. "Hortense Calisher: A Bibliography, 1948-1986." *Bulletin of Bibliography* 45.1 (March 1988): 40-50.

Sound coverage of writings both by and about Calisher through 1986. Primary coverage is arranged by publication format and genre, then sub-arranged chronologically. Enumerative treatment of books records variant editions and analyzes contents of short story collections, indicating original and subsequent publication of individual pieces. Secondary items not annotated.

CAMPBELL, JOHN W., JR. (1910-)

*150. Tuck, Donald. In *John W. Campbell: An Australian Tribute*. Ed. John Bangsund. Canberra: Ronald E. Graham and John Bangsund, 1972.

Item 46 reports Tuck's bibliography lists books, series, and short fiction. Treatment, however, omits edited books and nonfiction.

CAPOTE, TRUMAN (1924-1984)

151. Wall, Richard J., and Carl L. Craycraft. "A Checklist of Works about Truman Capote." *Bulletin of the New York Public Library* 71 (March 1967): 165-172.

    Unannotated record of secondary references to both scholarly and popular commentary on Capote. Fully superseded by Item 156.

152. Bryer, Jackson R. "Truman Capote: A Bibliography." In *Truman Capote, 'In Cold Blood': A Critical Handbook*. Ed. Irving Malin. Belmont, Calif.: Wadsworth Publishing Co., 1968, 239-269.

    Extensive primary and secondary record of English-language materials through 1966. Largely unannotated list of reviews and criticism is especially good for newspaper articles. Essentially superseded by Item 156.

153. Vanderwerken, David L. "Truman Capote, 1943-1968: A Critical Bibliography." *Bulletin of Bibliography* 27.3 (July-September 1970): 57-60, 71.

    Enumerative primary and unannotated secondary record through 1968. The abbreviated treatment of writings by Capote lists English-language versions only and limits periodical items to uncollected pieces. Coverage of commentary on Capote excludes most newspaper and popular magazine articles. Superseded by Item 156, except for alphabetical arrangement.

154. Starosciak, Kenneth. *Truman Capote: A Checklist*. New Brighton, Minn.: Starosciak, 1974.

    Pamphlet-length record of primary and secondary references. Extensive scope but coverage is unannotated and sometimes uneven; now superseded by Item 156.

155. Bonnet, Jean-Marie. "Truman Capote: A Selected Bibliography." *Delta* 11 (1980): 89-104.

Useful for providing citations to Capote's 1979 periodical publications; otherwise redundant with Item 156.

156. Stanton, Robert J. *Truman Capote: A Primary and Secondary Bibliography*. Boston: G.K. Hall, 1980.

Scrupulous account of materials by and about Capote into 1978. Chronologically arranged, enumerative coverage of primary sources furnishes very detailed records of both the numerous foreign-language translations of Capote's work and the frequent reprintings of his shorter pieces. The chronological secondary section also attempts to be exhaustive, though European and other foreign reviews are notably absent; contents notes accompany all secondary entries.

157. Wilson, Robert A. "Truman Capote: A Bibliographical Checklist." *American Book Collector* ns 1.4 (July-August 1980): 8-15.

Descriptive information sufficient for accurate bibliographical identification of Capote's separate publications, including books, contributions to books, and dramatic scripts. Chronological arrangement, with coverage into 1980.

CHAPELL, FRED (1936-)

158. Kibler, James Everett, Jr. "A Fred Chapell Bibliography, 1963-1983." *Mississippi Quarterly* 37.1 (Winter 1983-1984): 63-88.

Furnishes detailed coverage of works by Chapell and selected treatment of writings about him through 1983. Primary references are arranged chronologically within genre and format of publication. Enumerative account of Chapell's novels records variant editions, including translations into French; checklist of his stories notes reprintings and translations subsequent to original periodical publication. Unannotated secondary section excludes reviews, focusing instead on more substantial biographical and critical pieces.

CHEEVER, JOHN (1912-1982)

159. Coates, Dennis. "John Cheever: A Checklist, 1930-1978." *Bulletin of Bibliography* 36.1 (January-March 1979): 1-13, 49.

   Record of primary and secondary references through 1978. Detailed chronological list of Cheever's periodical publications scrupulously registers subsequent collection in books and anthologies. Unannotated handling of reviews and critical commentary on Cheever largely superseded by Item 161.

160. Trakas, Deno. "John Cheever: An Annotated Secondary Bibliography (1943-1978)." *Resources for American Literary Study* 9.2 (Autumn 1979): 181-199.

   Chronological arrangement, depth of coverage, and scope closely parallel Item 161, which supersedes Trakas's record, except for the interest of the annotations.

161. Bosha, Francis J. *John Cheever: A Reference Guide*. Boston: G.K. Hall, 1981.

   Chronological coverage of writings by and about Cheever through 1979. Enumerative primary section records different editions of separate publications, including translations, but coverage of periodical pieces is limited to uncollected nonfiction. Treatment of reviews in secondary section is deliberately representative, especially with regard to newspaper notices; otherwise, all entries are accompanied by thorough contents notes.

162. Coates, Dennis. "A Cheever Bibliography Supplement, 1978-1981." In *Critical Essays on John Cheever*. Ed. R.G. Collins. Boston: G.K. Hall, 1982, 279-285.

Supplements and updates Item 159, including primary and secondary items omitted as well as those newly published into 1981. Unannotated but thorough, especially for English-language materials.

163. Chaney, Bev, Jr., and William Burton. "John Cheever: A Bibliographical Checklist." *American Book Collector* ns 7.8 (August 1986): 22-31.

Chronological, informally descriptive account of Cheever's separate publications as well as those composite books to which he has contributed, into 1986. Sufficient information is provided for all entries to distinguish variant editions and identify first issues. No periodical or secondary references included.

CLEMENT, HAL (1922-)

164. Drumm, Chris. *A Hal Clement Checklist.* Polk City, Iowa: Chris Drumm, 1982. Rev. ed. in preparation, San Bernardino, Calif.: Borgo Press.

Chronological account of Clement's writings into 1982. Enumerative treatment of books records first as well as subsequent editions along with their total pagination and original publication prices. Entries for short stories and other contributions to periodicals list their reprintings in Clement's own collections and in anthologies.

COLLINS, MICHAEL (1924-)

165. "Bibliographie de Michael Collins." *Les Durs à cuire* 2 (March 1982): 24-31.

Chronological coverage into 1982 of Collins' novels and short stories, published under his own name and various pseudonyms. Enumerative treatment of books supplemented by photographic reproductions of selected covers. No secondary references but French editions are listed.

COOVER, ROBERT (1932-)

166. [Hertzel, Leo J.] "A Coover Checklist." *Critique* 11.3 (1969): 23-24.

   Enumerative record of Coover's writings through 1968, largely superseded by Item 167, except for coverage of subsequently collected stories, which are not individually noted by McCaffery.

167. McCaffery, Larry. "Donald Barthelme, Robert Coover, William H. Gass: Three Checklists." *Bulletin of Bibliography* 31.1 (July-September 1974): 101-106, esp. 103-104.

   Enumerative primary and unannotated secondary coverage of published writings through 1972. Printing history of Coover's periodical pieces not traced; list of critical responses focuses on major sources and excludes local newspaper reviews.

168. Blachowicz, Camille. "GLR/Bibliography: Contemporary Midwest Writers Series, No. 2, Robert Coover." *Great Lakes Review* 3.1 (Summer 1976): 69-73.

   Chronologically arranged primary coverage accompanied by alphabetically ordered secondary record, into 1975. Works by Coover presented by genre, with separate sections for his books, stories, and nonfiction.

169. McCaffery, Larry. "Robert Coover (b. 1932)." In *The Metafictional Muse: The Works of Robert Coover, Donald Barthelme, and William H. Gass*. Pittsburgh: Univ. of Pittsburgh Press, 1982, 285-287.

   Extends coverage of Item 167 into 1981, but secondary scope is limited to critical essays and excludes reviews.

170. Allensworth, J. "Robert Coover: A Bibliographic Chronicle of Primary Materials." *Bulletin of Bibliography* 41.2 (June 1984): 61-63.

Chronologically arranged, enumerative checklist of writings by Coover into 1983. Includes previously unrecorded reviews and essays by Coover and also notes reprintings of individual periodical pieces.

CRAIG, JONATHAN (1919-)

*171. Schleret, Jean-Jacques. "Entretien avec Jonathan Craig (Frank E. Smith)." *Enigmatika* 24 (July 1983): 61-66.

Item 2 indicates that the bibliography that accompanies this interview lists both English-language and French publications, novels, and short stories.

CREWS, HARRY (1935-)

172. Hargraves, Michael. *Harry Crews: A First Bibliography*. San Francisco: Michael Hargraves, 1981.

Early, now superseded version of Item 174.

173. Gann, Daniel H. "Harry Crews: A Bibliography." *Bulletin of Bibliography* 39.3 (September 1982): 139-145.

Enumerative, chronological checklist of works by Crews followed by unannotated record of secondary sources. Essentially superseded by Item 174.

174. Hargraves, Michael. *Harry Crews: A Bibliography*. Westport, Ct.: Meckler, 1986.

Fully descriptive treatment of works by Crews, supplemented by unannotated lists of reviews of his books as well as by an idiosyncratically annotated record of articles about him. Coverage into 1985, with scope of primary record extending to blurbs, screenplays, and videos. Physical account of Crews' separate publications complemented by photographs of title pages of first editions.

CROSSEN, KEN (1910-)

*175. Miller, Don. "Kendall Foster Crossen Bibliography." *Mystery Nook* 12 (June 1979): B1-B24.

Item 2 reports that the primary sections are arranged by title, pseudonym/author's name, principal characters, magazine, and publisher; secondary sources are also recorded.

DANIELS, NORMAN A. (-)

*176. Wills, Murray. "The Amazing Norman A. Daniels." *Echoes* 1.4 (February 1983): 7-15.

Item 2 indicates this article concludes with a checklist of Daniels' publications based on his own records; the article itself furnishes detailed information on series to which Daniels has contributed.

DAVENPORT, GUY (1927-)

177. Burton, William. "Guy Davenport: A Bibliographic Checklist." *American Book Collector* ns 5.2 (March-April 1984): 37-46.

Provides chronologically ordered, abbreviated descriptive treatment of both Davenport's separate publications and the books to which he has contributed, into 1984. Supplemental notes allow differentiation between variant editions and issues.

DAVIDSON, AVRAM (1923-)

*178. Grant, Richard. "A Bibliography of Avram Davidson." *Megavore* 9 (June 1980): 4-20.

Reported in the 1980 volume of *The Year's Scholarship in Science Fiction, Fantasy, and Horror Literature* (Kent, Ohio: Kent State Univ. Press, 1983) to list all short story appearances, nonfiction articles, verse, edited anthologies, and books, including reprint data.

DAWSON, FIELDING (1930-)

179. Butterick, George F. *Fielding Dawson: A Checklist of His Writings*. Storrs: Univ. of Connecticut Library, 1976.

Exemplary coverage of writings by and about Dawson into 1976. The enumerative presentation of books and other separate publications includes supplementary information about publishing history of individual items. Treatment of periodical contributions extends to their subsequent reprinting. Secondary citations are not annotated.

DE CAMP, L. SPRAGUE (1907-)

180. Laughlin, Charlotte, and Daniel J.H. Levack. *De Camp: An L. Sprague de Camp Bibliography*. San Francisco and Columbia, Pa.: Underwood/Miller, 1983.

Provides an exhaustive inventory of De Camp's published writings through mid-1982. Primary coverage is presented in separate, alphabetically organized sections for books, edited books, nonbook appearances, translations, and miscellaneous items. Books are accorded informal but thorough bibliographic descriptions, extending to variant editions and foreign-language translations. These physical accounts are supplemented by numerous photographic reproductions of wrappers and dust jackets; each item is also accompanied by a plot summary. Similar contents notes are furnished for all De Camp's contributions to periodicals; reprintings, translations, and anthologizations of these magazine pieces are also carefully noted.

DELANY, SAMUEL R. (1942-)

181. Peplow, Michael W., and Robert S. Bravard. *Samuel R. Delany: A Primary and Secondary Bibliography, 1962-1979*. Boston: G.K. Hall, 1980.

Scrupulously thorough coverage of published writings by and about Delany into 1979. Exhaustive enumerative treatment of Delany's separate publications, including foreign-language translations, is supplemented by informal notes about their publishing history. Record of Delany's nonfiction books and periodical contributions is well annotated, as is the checklist of reviews and articles about him.

182. ----------. "Samuel R. Delany: A Selective Primary and Secondary Bibliography, 1977-1983." *Black American Literature Forum* 18.2 (Summer 1984): 75-77.

Supplements Item 181, updating the Delany record through 1983. Same careful style continues, though secondary entries are not annotated here. The checklist's selectivity is a function not of deliberate choice but rather stems from a frank recognition of the inevitable limitations of a contemporary science fiction bibliography.

DE LA TORRE, LILLIAN (1902-)

183. Purcell, James Mark. "Lillian de la Torre, Preliminary Bibliography: Blood on the Periwigs." *Mystery Readers Newsletter* (July-August 1971): 25-27.

Furnishes an inventory of De la Torre's fiction and plays through 1960, including detailed record of the original periodical publication of stories later collected in the books for which she was then best known.

DELILLO, DON (1936-)

184. Y[oung], J[ames] D[ean]. "A Don DeLillo Checklist." *Critique* 20.1 (1978): 25-26.

Presents works by and about DeLillo through 1977. Primary coverage treats the novels enumeratively, noting variant editions as well as sections previously published in periodicals; DeLillo's magazine fiction is recorded in a separate section.

Secondary coverage consists predominantly of unannotated list of reviews that appeared in major national newspapers and journals.

185. LeClair, Tom. "Bibliography." In *In the Loop: Don DeLillo and the Systems Novel*. Urbana: Univ. of Illinois Press, 1987, 237-240.

Updates Item 184 into 1986, with particular attention to critical commentary exclusive of reviews.

DEMING, RICHARD (1915-1983)

*186. "Bibliographie" and "Filmographie." *Les Durs à cuire* 7 (n.d.): 25-40, 41-43.

Item 2 cites this French crime fiction magazine by its English title, *Hard Boiled Dicks*, and reports that this number, featuring Deming, includes checklists of both his publications and film adaptations.

DE VRIES, PETER (1910-)

187. Bowden, Edwin T. "Peter De Vries--The First Thirty Years: A Bibliography, 1934-1964." *Texas Studies in Literature and Language* 6.1 (Spring 1964): 543-570.

Full descriptive treatment of De Vries' books and those to which he contributed, along with detailed treatment of his periodical publications. Fully superseded by Item 188.

188. ----------. *Peter De Vries: A Bibliography 1934-1977*. Austin: Humanities Research Center, Univ. of Texas, 1978.

An exacting, detailed record of De Vries' published writings through 1977. Full bibliographic descriptions of separately published books, including composite volumes with original contributions by him. Subsequent reprintings of De Vries' periodical pieces noted, as are revisions between different appearances of individual works.

189. Straayer, T.A. "Peter De Vries: A Bibliography of Secondary Sources, 1940-1981." *Bulletin of Bibliography* 39.3 (September 1982): 146-169.

    Thoroughly annotated account of commentary on De Vries through 1981. Separate sections for biographical information, general criticism, interviews, and book reviews. Excludes reviews from small circulation magazines and local newspapers. Otherwise seeks to be comprehensive.

DICK, PHILIP K. (1928-1982)

190. McNelly, Willis E. "Manuscripts and Papers at Fullerton." *Science-Fiction Studies* 2.2 (March 1975): 4-5.

    Furnishes a rough census of the document boxes containing Dick's published and unpublished manuscripts, letters, and other papers housed in the library at California State University, Fullerton.

191. Mullen, R.D. "The Books, Stories, Essays." *Science-Fiction Studies* 2.2 (March 1975): 5-8.

    Chronological checklists into 1974 covering the American and British editions of Dick's books as well as his stories and articles first published in anthologies. Reprintings of the same edition are not recorded.

192. Patten, Fred. "Bibliography." In *Philip K. Dick: Electric Shepherd*. Ed. Bruce Gillespie. Melbourne: Norstrilia Press, 1975.

    Chronological record of the first periodical appearances of Dick's short stories and novellas from 1952-1974, followed by an enumerative chronology of the various American editions of his novels and collections.

193. Levack, Daniel J.H. *PDK: A Philip K. Dick Bibliography*. San Francisco and Columbia, Pa.: Underwood/Miller, 1981. Rev. ed. Westport, Ct.: Meckler, 1988.

Exhaustive account of Dick's work through mid-1981, divided into separate, alphabetically arranged sections for books, stories, unpublished manuscripts, and other media. Enumerative treatment of the books includes informal physical descriptions and careful registration of variant editions, extending to foreign-language versions; contents notes accompany each book entry and photographic reproductions of dust jackets, wrappers, or title pages further supplement the coverage of most individual titles. Plot summaries are also provided for all short story entries, which note as well subsequent printings in both other magazines and collections. Also present are a highly selective, unannotated list of secondary references and a chronology of Dick's writings that complements the bibliography's alphabetical organization. While intended to be comprehensive for both English and foreign-language materials, Levack acknowledges the probable omission of non-English imprints. Revised edition maintains the same organization and structure, while extending coverage through late 1984.

194. Tymn, Marshall B. "Philip K. Dick: A Bibliography." In *Philip K. Dick*. Ed. Martin Harry Greenberg and Joseph D. Olander. New York: Taplinger, 1983, 241-248.

Alphabetically arranged checklist of items by and about Dick into 1981 that is comprehensive in scope but selective in coverage. Useful principally for its updating of secondary coverage; otherwise, introduces little new bibliographic information.

195. Mackey, Douglas A. "Selected Bibliography." In *Philip K. Dick*. Twayne's United States Authors Series 533. Boston: Twayne, 1988, 133-151.

Distinguished by its thorough coverage of the secondary literature, with references into 1987. Each of the critical items entered in the separate sections for books, interviews, and articles is accompanied by a brief but quite useful annotation.

DICKSON, GORDON R. (1923-)

196. Thompson, Raymond H. *Gordon R. Dickson: A Primary and Secondary Bibliography*. Boston: G.K. Hall, 1983.

Exhaustive account of works by Dickson and writings about him into 1981. Chronological, enumerative treatment of primary materials divides itself into separate sections for fiction, nonfiction, and miscellaneous media, with informal notes explaining bibliographical connections among different items and recording reprintings. Secondary coverage fully annotated.

DIDION, JOAN (1934-)

197. Jacobs, Fred Rue. *Joan Didion: Bibliography*. Keene, Calif.: Loop Press, 1977.

Thorough but unannotated checklist of published writings by and about Didion into 1977. Jacobs's information has been essentially incorporated in Item 198, except for his coverage of motion picture reviews of screenplays Didion co-authored.

198. Olendorf, Donna. "Joan Didion: A Working Checklist, 1955-1980." *Bulletin of Bibliography* 38.1 (January-March 1981): 32-44.

Careful record of writings by and about Didion into 1980. Enumerative primary treatment covers early journalism (exclusive of unsigned pieces), lists translations, and notes subsequent reprintings of periodical contributions. Secondary sections are thorough but unannotated. Except for general and biographical criticism, arrangement is chronological.

DILLARD, ANNIE (1945-)

199. Scheick, William J. "A Bibliography of Writings by Annie Dillard." In *Contemporary American Women Writers: Narrative Strategies*. Ed. Catherine Rainwater and William J. Scheick. Lexington: Univ. Press of Kentucky, 1985, 64-67.

Presents Dillard's work chronologically within genre, with references as late as 1984. The separate lists of her uncollected short stories, poems, and nonfiction pieces are especially useful. No secondary references.

DISCH, THOMAS M. (1940-)

200. Nee, Dave. *Thomas M. Disch: A Preliminary Bibliography*. Berkeley, Calif.: Other Change of Hobbit, 1982.

Highly informative account of Disch's published writings through mid-1981, with separate, alphabetically arranged lists of his books and edited anthologies as well as of his original periodical contributions of fiction, nonfiction, and poetry. Enumerative treatment of books records variant English-language editions. Coverage of magazine pieces carefully notes subsequent republication.

201. Drumm, Chris. *A Tom Disch Checklist*. Polk City, Iowa: Chris Drumm, 1983.

Chronological account of Disch's work through 1982, with additional citations into 1983. Enumerative treatment of books notes first as well as subsequent editions, recording both total pagination and original publication price of each edition. Handling of short stories and other contributions to periodicals carefully lists reprintings.

DODSON, OWEN (1914-)

202. Hatch, James V., Douglas A.M. Ward, and Joe Weixlmann. "The Rungs of a Powerful Long Ladder: An Owen Dodson Bibliography." *Black American Literature Forum* 14.2 (Summer 1980): 60-68.

Exhaustively detailed coverage of published writings by and about Dodson into 1980. Primary works are presented chronologically according to genre, with reviews interpolated without annotation. In addition to sections tracing the printing histories of Dodson's novels and short stories, there are also sections for his poetry, plays, reviews and essays, interviews, and recordings.

DONLEAVY, J.P. (1926-)

203. Madden, David W. "A Bibliography of J.P. Donleavy." *Bulletin of Bibliography* 39.3 (September 1982): 170-178.

Provides record of writings by and about Donleavy into 1981. Enumerative primary treatment is arranged by genre and indicates variant American and British editions as well as republications of periodical pieces. Unannotated secondary coverage focuses on references in the national magazines of the United States and Britain.

DOWELL, COLEMAN (1925-1985)

204. Kuehl, John, and Linda Kandel Kuehl. "The Achievement of Coleman Dowell: A Bibliographical Essay." *Review of Contemporary Fiction* 7.3 (Fall 1987): 227-232.

Narrative account of works by and about Dowell into 1987. Recounts Dowell's publishing history, indicating the journals and newspapers to which he contributed his short fiction and reviews as well as explaining the compositional sequence of his novels and their relation to existing manuscript resources. Secondary coverage summarizes Dowell's critical reception but does not provide detailed bibliographic information about all items to which references are made.

DUBUS, ANDRÉ (1936-)

205. "Bibliographie sélective: Oeuvres d'André Dubus." *Delta* 24 (February 1987): 151-156.

Checklist of works by and about Dubus into 1986. Chronological, enumerative account of books records translations; alphabetical treatment of stories in periodicals notes republication in collections. Dubus's interviews and nonfiction pieces entered separately, followed by a brief, unannotated list of critical articles. No secondary reviews.

EASTLAKE, WILLIAM (1917-)

206. McPheron, William. "William Eastlake: A Checklist." *Review of Contemporary Fiction* 3.1 (Spring 1983): 93-105.

Thorough record of published writings by and about Eastlake into 1982. Enumerative account of primary items registers variant editions and translations of separate publications and also traces subsequent printings of periodical pieces. Secondary coverage includes brief discussions of Eastlake but is unannotated.

207. Lewis, Linda K. "William Eastlake." *Bulletin of Bibliography* 41.1 (March 1984): 6-11.

Provides enumerative primary and unannotated secondary treatment of published Eastlake references through 1982. Updates and occasionally supplements Item 206 but is generally less complete for materials appearing prior to 1982.

ELKIN, STANLEY (1930-)

208. McCaffery, Larry. "Stanley Elkin: A Bibliography, 1957-1977." *Bulletin of Bibliography* 34.2 (April-June 1977): 73-76.

Thorough checklist of published works by and about Elkin to 1977. Primary sections are enumerative; secondary record is unannotated.

209. Bargen, Doris G. "Bibliography." In *The Fiction of Stanley Elkin*. Frankfurt: Peter D. Lang, 1980, 305-329, esp. 305-312.

This two-part checklist treats writings by and about Elkin through 1977. Enumerative, chronologically arranged primary section notes variant editions of books and provides detailed coverage of the republication of pieces originally appearing in periodicals. Unannotated secondary part emphasizes reviews in national magazines, omitting items from local newspapers. Updates and complements Item 208.

210. Chénetier, Marc. "Stanley Elkin: Bibliographie Sélective." *Delta* 20 (February 1985): 207-214.

Sound coverage of primary texts into 1983, reliably updating the coverage of Elkin's own writings offered in Items 208 and 209, including more recent periodical items and interviews. Selective list of critical commentary.

ELLISON, HARLAN (1934-)

211. Swigart, Leslie Kay. *Harlan Ellison: A Bibliographical Checklist*. Dallas: Williams Publishing, 1973.

Very detailed, thorough record of Ellison's work into 1973. Abbreviated descriptive treatment of his books is supplemented by photographs of their covers; both variant English and foreign-language editions are described. Other sections list Ellison's produced film and television scripts, his periodical fiction, articles and essays, introductions and afterwords, reviews by him of works in various media, published letters, interviews, and fanzines edited by him. Many entries accompanied by brief explanatory and bibliographical notes. Good index includes Ellison's numerous pseudonyms. Secondary materials are not within Swigart's scope.

212. ----------. "Harlan Ellison: An F & SF Checklist." *Magazine of Fantasy and Science Fiction* 53.1 (July 1977): 80-89.

Awkwardly compact but highly informative account of Ellison's science fiction and nonfiction writings through 1975. Chronological coverage of books written and edited by Ellison includes contents notes and variant editions. Record of his fiction contributed to periodicals is alphabetical by story title, while the account of nonfiction lists only the titles of relevant periodicals and books. Pieces in fanzines and college periodicals, though numerous, are omitted. No secondary references.

ELLISON, RALPH (1914-)

213. Lillard, R. Stewart. "A Ralph Waldo Ellison Bibliography (1914-1967)." *American Book Collector* 19.3 (November 1968): 18-22.

Chronological, enumerative coverage of Ellison's writings through 1967, including careful account of reprintings of original publications in collected works and anthologies. Especially valuable for identifying Ellison's earliest work, including short stories and book reviews.

214. Polsgrove, Carol. "Addenda to 'A Ralph Waldo Ellison Bibliography' 1914-1968." *American Book Collector* 20.3 (November-December 1969): 11-12.

Supplements and updates Item 213 by chronologically listing items inadvertently omitted by Lillard, including various fugitive pieces, and extending coverage into 1968.

215. Baily, Lugene, and Frank E. Moorer. "A Selected Checklist of Materials by and about Ralph Ellison." *Black World* 20.2 (December 1970): 126-130.

Abbreviated coverage of primary and secondary references into 1970. Chronological list of works by Ellison includes his early periodical contributions. Unannotated record of writings about him extends to citations of unpublished doctoral dissertations.

216. Benoit, Bernard, and Michel Fabre. "A Bibliography of Ralph Ellison's Published Writings." *Studies in Black Literature* 2.3 (Autumn 1971): 25-28.

Enumerative checklist of primary materials to June 1971, based on Items 213 and 214 and both supplementing and updating Lillard and Polsgrove's coverage. Arranged chronologically within genres, including separate sections for fiction, literary criticism, art and music criticism, and essays, lectures, and interviews. Brief contents and reprinting notes throughout. Some pre-1967 references from Items 213 and 214 that were inadvertently omitted.

217. Covo, Jacqueline. "Ralph Waldo Ellison: Bibliographic Essays and Finding List of American Criticism, 1952-1964." *College Language Association Journal* 15.2 (December 1971): 171-196.

Thorough record of American critical and biographical commentary on Ellison through 1964. Very useful narrative evaluation of these materials precedes the checklist and serves as annotations.

218. ----------. "Ralph Ellison in France: Bibliographic Essays and Checklist of French Criticism, 1954-1971." *College Language Association Journal* 16.4 (June 1973): 519-526.

Narrative account of critical commentary on Ellison in France through 1971 precedes enumerative checklist of secondary references.

219. ----------. *The Blinking Eye: Ralph Waldo Ellison and His American, French, German, and Italian Critics 1952-1971.* Scarecrow Author Bibliographies 18. Metuchen, N.J.: Scarecrow Press, 1974.

Updates and expands scope of Items 217 and 218, while also extending analogous coverage to the German and Italian receptions of Ellison. Following essays that summarize the critical commentary in each country, the individual national checklists are arranged alphabetically within subdivisions by type of publication. A provisional record of reviews and criticism printed in the British Commonwealth serves as an appendix.

220. Giza, Joanne. "Ralph Ellison." In *Black American Writers: Bibliographical Essays.* Vol. 2. Ed. M. Thomas Inge, Maurice Duke, and Jackson R. Bryer. New York: St. Martin's Press, 1978, 47-71.

Careful narrative and critical review of secondary materials into 1976. Though a selective account of scholarship and commentary on Ellison, it serves as a useful bibliographical overview.

221. Weixlmann, Joe, and John O'Banion. "A Checklist of Ellison Criticism, 1972-1978." *Black American Literature Forum* 12.2 (Summer 1978): 51-55.

Deliberately designed to update the coverage of Item 219. Furnishes alphabetically arranged, unannotated record of critical commentary on Ellison into 1978. Also includes citations to the secondary literature prior to 1972, which Covo omitted. Range of references is very wide, including unpublished dissertations, European publications, and even some instructor's manuals.

ERDRICH, LOUISE (1954-)

222. "Louise Erdrich: A S.A.I.L. Bibliography." *Studies in American Indian Literature* 3.1 (Winter 1985): 37-41.

Checklist of primary materials, including work-in-progress, with references into 1985. Periodical contributions are listed chronologically, books treated enumeratively. Neither references to reviews of Erdrich's novels nor other citations of secondary literature.

FARMER, PHILIP JOSÉ (1918-)

223. Knapp, Lawrence J. *The First Editions of Philip José Farmer.* Menlo Park, Calif.: David G. Turner, 1976.

Coverage of works by and about Farmer into 1976, with separate sections for books, uncollected short stories, and secondary references, including interviews. Enumerative, chronological presentation of books records first editions only but does carefully note previous versions or publication of their contents in periodicals. List of stories is alphabetical. Secondary references exclude reviews, concentrating on more substantive biographical and critical pieces. Item 40 above cites a revised edition of Knapp's bibliography (West Linn, Oregon: Starmont, 1980), which was not seen.

224. Wymer, Thomas L. "Speculative Fiction, Bibliographies, and Philip José Farmer." *Extrapolation* 18.1 (December 1976): 59-72.

Furnishes a chronological record of Farmer's science fiction writings through 1976, with indications of items forthcoming in 1977. Enumerative treatment of books registers variant editions. Republication in collected volumes and anthologies of stories originally printed in periodicals is carefully noted, though pagination is not reported. The occasional title changes of individual works as well as pseudonymous pieces are also recorded.

225. Whitney, Paul. "Philip José Farmer: A Checklist." *Science Fiction Collector* 5 (September 1977): 4-20.

Arranges primary coverage of Farmer's work into three sections for his books, for stories, articles, and verse first published in periodicals, and for miscellaneous items, such as introductions, interviews, and speeches. All sections are organized alphabetically, with citations into 1977. Records American and British editions, excludes foreign-language translations, but does reproduce numerous covers; entries for the first appearances of magazine pieces are supplemented by lists of selected reprintings. Omits letters to fanzines.

FOOTE, SHELBY (1916-)

226. Kibler, James E., Jr. "Shelby Foote: A Bibliography." *Mississippi Quarterly* 24.4 (Fall 1971): 437-465.

Exemplary account of works by Foote and selective record of writings about him into 1970. Chronologically arranged primary section features full descriptive coverage of Foote's books--with supplementary notes on their publishing histories--followed by separate lists of his short stories, reviews, lectures, and interviews. The occasionally annotated secondary coverage is limited to more significant articles and reviews.

227. [Richard, Claude]. "Bibliographie" [in special number devoted to Foote]. *Delta* 4 (May 1977): 181-189.

Though predominantly a selected, enumerative version of Item 226, this checklist does update Kibler's record of primary materials into 1975 and also furnishes an unannotated record of the French reception of translated versions of Foote's work.

FORD, JESSE HILL (1928-)

228. White, Helen. *Jesse Hill Ford: An Annotated Check List of His Published Works and of His Papers*. Mississippi Valley Collection Bulletin 7. Memphis, Tenn.: Memphis State Univ., 1974.

Detailed inventory of printed and manuscript materials by Ford, followed by selective treatment of published writings about him into 1974. Primary coverage is organized chronologically within genre and publication format. Enumerative account of Ford's novels includes a description of plot and an explanation of each text's relation to his other fiction. Contents notes also accompany entries in the separate lists of his short stories and his nonfiction pieces. Brief, annotated secondary section concentrates on biographical and critical articles, excluding reviews. Descriptions of manuscript materials encompass both their physical aspects and their contents.

FRANCIS, H. E. (1924-)

229. Sola, Graciela de. "H. E. Francis: Bibliography." *DeKalb Literary Arts Journal* 1.3 (Spring 1967): 49-51.

Checklist of works by Francis through 1966. Bibliographical information incorporated in Item 230.

230. "H. E. Francis: Bibliography." *DeKalb Literary Arts Journal* 4.2 (1970): 83-87.

Primary and secondary coverage through 1969. Presents Francis' published writings chronologically within genre, including detailed listing of his short stories contributed to periodicals as well as his reviews and translations. Brief, unannotated list of writings about him.

GADDIS, WILLIAM (1922-)

231. Kuehl, John, and Steven Moore. "Bibliography." In *In Recognition of William Gaddis*. Syracuse: Syracuse Univ. Press, 1984, 199-206.

Records writings by and about Gaddis through 1983. Enumerative primary checklist covers periodical publications; secondary treatment briefly annotates items, except dissertations; reviews of Gaddis's books are excluded entirely.

GAINES, ERNEST J. (1933-)

232. Rowell, Charles H. "Ernest J. Gaines: A Checklist, 1964-1978." *Calalloo* 1.3 (May 1978): 125-131.

Useful but provisional record of writings by and about Gaines into 1978. Enumerative treatment of Gaines' novels supplemented by list of interviews with him. Unannotated secondary coverage includes separate sections for general studies and reviews, the latter focusing on more prominent, mainstream national magazines.

GARDNER, JOHN (1933-1982)

233. Dillon, David A. "John C. Gardner: A Bibliography." *Bulletin of Bibliography* 34.2 (April-June 1977): 86-89, 104.

Primary and secondary checklist developed exclusively from standard indexes. Fully superseded by Items 234 and 236.

234. Howell, John M. *John Gardner: A Bibliographical Profile*. Carbondale: Southern Illinois Univ. Press, 1980.

Thorough record of writings both by and about Gardner into 1979. Exhaustive primary coverage arranges itself by genre of publication and includes such miscellaneous categories as blurbs, cartoons, playbills, and radio scripts. Abbreviated bibliographical descriptions are supplemented by numerous photographs of title pages. Unannotated secondary section lists reviews and more general criticism separately.

235. Hamilton, Lee T. "John Gardner: A Bibliographical Update." In *John Gardner: True Art, Moral Art*. Ed. Beatrice Mendez-Egle and James M. Haule. Living Author Series 5. Edinburg, Texas: Pan American Univ., School of Humanities, 1983, 113-132.

Designed to update coverage of Item 234 from 1979 into 1982. Chronological enumeration of primary items and unannotated record of secondary references are sound for the years treated but are fully superseded by Item 236.

236. Morace, Robert A. *John Gardner: An Annotated Secondary Bibliography*. Garland Reference Library of the Humanities 434. New York: Garland, 1984.

Scrupulous coverage of secondary sources into 1983, preceded by a generously annotated list of Gardner's interviews and speeches, including newspaper accounts of public appearances. Separate, chronologically ordered sections for reviews both of books by Gardner and of those to which he contributed, as well as a section for articles and notices other than reviews. All entries are thoroughly annotated. A final section records primary material not cited, or incorrectly cited in Item 234.

GARRETT, GEORGE (1929-)

237. Garrett, George, Thomas L. McHaney, and James B. Meriwether. "A Checklist of the Writings of George Garrett." *Princeton University Library Chronicle* 25.1 (Autumn 1963): 33-39.

Thorough, enumerative treatment of work by Garrett, including unpublished scripts, into late 1963.

238. *George Palmer Garrett: A Bibliography and Index of His Published Works and Criticism of Them*. Potsdam, N.Y.: Frederick W. Crumb Library, State Univ. College, 1968.

Primary and secondary checklist into 1968. Enumerative treatment of books and unannotated presentation of other materials. Citations derived from standard indexes only.

239. Dillard, R.H.W. "George Garrett: A Checklist of His Writings." *Mill Mountain Review* (Summer 1971): 221-234.

Coverage of primary materials into 1971, including an enumerative account of Garrett's books, a list of his contributions to periodicals--without, however, recording their later appearances in collections and anthologies--and an inventory of his unpublished screenplays.

240. Wright, Stuart. "George Garrett: A Bibliographic Chronicle, 1947-1980." *Bulletin of Bibliography* 38.1 (January-March 1981): 6-19, 25.

Exacting account of both primary and secondary printed sources through 1980. Section treating works by Garrett is arranged chronologically, with collected and republished appearances of individual pieces regularly recorded. Unannotated treatment of commentary on Garrett.

GASS, WILLIAM H. (1924-)

241. McCaffery, Larry. "Donald Barthelme, Robert Coover, and William Gass: Three Checklists." *Bulletin of Bibliography* 31.3 (July-September 1974): 101-106, esp. 104-106.

Enumerative primary and unannotated secondary coverage of published work through 1972. Superseded by Item 243.

242. French, Ned. "Bibliography." *Iowa Review* 7.1 (Winter 1976): 106-107.

Chronological list of Gass' publications through 1975. Superseded by Item 243.

243. McCaffery, Larry. "A William H. Gass Bibliography." *Critique* 18.1 (1976): 59-66.

Detailed record of published writings by and about Gass into 1976. Enumerative primary checklist notes variant editions and translations of books; also indicates the publishing history of periodical items. Secondary coverage is thorough but unannotated.

*244. Veley, Pamela Lee. "William H. Gass: A Critical Introduction and Bibliography." Diss. Pennsylvania State Univ. 1977.

Author reports in *Dissertation Abstracts International* 38 (1978): 7338A-39A, that the thesis includes a complete Gass bibliography, providing annotated coverage of primary texts as well as secondary discussions and reviews.

245. McCaffery, Larry. "William H. Gass (b.1924)." In *The Metafictional Muse: The Works of Robert Coover, Donald Barthelme, and William H. Gass*. Pittsburgh: Univ. of Pittsburgh Press, 1982, 290-293.

Updates coverage of Item 243 into 1981 but excludes all reviews of Gass' work.

GAULT, WILLIAM CAMPBELL (1910-)

246. "Bibliographie de William Campbell Gault." *Les Durs à cuire* 3 (June 1982): 21-33.

Combines chronological checklists of Gault's novels and short stories, including French translations. Magazine also cited as *Hard Boiled Dicks*.

GOULART, RON (1933-)

*247. Meech, Shirley. "Ron Goulart Checklist." *Comic Buyer's Guide* 16 (May 1982): 39-42.

Item 2 indicates this bibliography is particularly thorough in its treatment of Goulart's short stories.

GOVER, ROBERT (1929-)

248. Hargraves, Michael. *Robert Gover: A Descriptive Bibliography*. Westport, Ct.: Meckler, 1988.

Exhaustive account of writings by and about Gover into 1987. Chronological presentation of primary materials is arranged by publication format, with individual sections for original books, contributions to books, contributions to periodicals, translations, and miscellaneous items. Secondary coverage includes biographical and critical references.

GOYEN, WILLIAM (1915-1983)

249. Grimm, Clyde L., Jr. "William Goyen: A Bibliographic Chronicle." *Bulletin of Bibliography* 35.3 (July-September 1978): 123-131.

Thorough enumerative and chronological record of works by Goyen and extensive, unannotated list of reviews and criticism about him, into 1978. Primary coverage superseded by Item 251 but the international secondary sections remain very useful. French criticism noted but not the French periodical press reaction; account of American and British reviews is detailed, including some local newspaper pieces.

250. ----------, and Patrice Repusseau. "Bibliographies" [in a special number devoted to Goyen]. *Delta* 9 (November 1979): 219-250.

Updates into 1979 and expands coverage of Item 249. Enumerative, chronological treatment of Goyen's work is primarily subdivided by genre, and thus provides an alternative arrangement; basic bibliographic information is, however, fully incorporated in Item 251. Unannotated secondary checklists include English-language reviews omitted earlier by Grimm as well as featuring a separate section that extensively lists reviews from the French literary press.

251. Wright, Stuart. *William Goyen: A Descriptive Bibliography, 1938-1985*. Westport, Ct.: Meckler, 1986.

Scrupulously thorough and detailed coverage of Goyen's published writings through 1985. Full bibliographic descriptions of separately issued items. Treatment of Goyen's contributions to periodicals carefully notes variants between original magazine appearance and subsequent reprinting. Section on interviews provides brief contents notes.

GRAU, SHIRLEY ANN (1929-)

252. Grissom, Margaret S. "Shirley Ann Grau: A Checklist." *Bulletin of Bibliography* 28.3 (July-September 1971): 76-78.

Chronologically ordered, enumerative record of primary sources through 1968. Separate sections for books, short stories, and articles. Except for early contributions to Grau's college literary magazine, the checklist seeks to be comprehensive.

GREENBERG, ALVIN (1932-)

253. Baer, Joel H. "Alvin Greenberg: A Checklist of His Work, 1959-1985." *Literary Research* 11.1 (Winter 1986): 19-64.

Detailed, exhaustive coverage of writings by and about Greenberg through 1985, with references into 1986. Enumerative primary treatment is divided by genre, with separate chronological sections for Greenberg's novels and stories as well as for poetry, drama, criticism, and editorial work. There is also a brief, unannotated record of secondary references, which supplements the lists of reviews incorporated in the primary sections.

GUNN, JAMES (1923-)

254. Drumm, Chris. *A James Gunn Checklist*. Polk City, Iowa: Chris Drumm, 1984. Rev. ed. in preparation, San Bernardino, Calif.: Borgo Press.

Thorough chronological account of Gunn's works into 1984. Enumerative treatment of books registers first as well as subsequent editions and translations. Information includes total pagination and original publication price of each item. Handling of short stories and other contributions to periodicals carefully notes reprintings in Gunn's own collections and in anthologies. No references to the secondary literature.

GUTHRIE, A. B. (1901-)

255. Etulain, Richard W. "A.B. Guthrie: A Bibliography." *Western American Literature* 4.2 (Summer 1969): 133-138.

Account of writings by and about Guthrie includes citations into 1969. Primary coverage is arranged alphabetically in different genres, with enumerative treatment of books, followed by separate lists for periodical appearances of Guthrie's poetry, stories and essays, and reviews. Unannotated secondary section focuses on substantial critical discussions and excludes most reviews.

HANSEN, JOSEPH (1923-)

*256. Bibliographie de Joseph Hansen." *Les Durs à cuire* 4 (October 1982): 13-16.

Item 2 cites this French crime fiction magazine by its English title, *Hard Boiled Dicks*, and indicates that this special number featuring Hansen contains a bibliography of his work.

HARRISON, HARRY (1925-)

*257. Biamonti, Francesco. *Harry Harrison: Bibliographia (1951-1965)*. Trieste: Editoriale Libraria, 1965.

Described by Robert E. Briney and Edward Wood in their *SF Bibliographies: An Annotated Bibliography of Bibliographical Works on Science Fiction and Fantasy Fiction* (Chicago: Advent Publishers, 1972) as a nine-page alphabetical list of Harrison's stories, articles, and guest editorials through 1965, with brief annotations by Harrison himself. Information on variant editions, including foreign-language issues, is furnished. Biamonti's bibliography is also reported by Item 46.

HARRISON, JIM (1937-)

258. Colonnese, Tom. "Jim Harrison: A Checklist." *Bulletin of Bibliography* 39.3 (September 1982): 132-135.

> Coverage of published writings by and about Harrison through 1981. Primary materials are presented by genre, then subarranged chronologically. Enumerative treatment of novels, books of poetry, and anthologies. Lists of Harrison's periodical contributions as well as the unannotated record of secondary literature derive from standard indexes and bibliographic data bases, consequently omitting many little magazine items.

HAWKES, JOHN (1925-)

259. Bryer, Jackson R. "Two Bibliographies." *Critique* 6.2 (Fall 1963): 86-94, esp. 89-94.

> Checklist of writings by and about Hawkes, with references into 1963. Organized chronologically within genre, the primary coverage first enumerates books and their variant editions as well as their reviews, and then proceeds through separate lists to cover Hawkes's fiction, nonfiction, and poetry contributions to periodicals. Citations of secondary literature are not annotated.

260. Plung, Daniel. "John Hawkes: A Selected Bibliography, 1943-1975." *Critique* 17.3 (1976): 53-63.

> Useful, conveniently presented checklist of works by and about Hawkes through 1975. Enumerative primary coverage and unannotated secondary treatment superseded by Item 264, except for dimension of selectivity.

261. Hryciw, Carol A. *John Hawkes: An Annotated Bibliography.* Scarecrow Author Bibliographies 32. Metuchen, N.J.: Scarecrow Press, 1977.

Provides scrupulously thorough coverage of English-language publications both by and about Hawkes, supplemented by some foreign-language materials and references to unpublished academic theses. Enumerative account of separately issued primary texts, including translations; record of contributions to periodicals notes their relation to subsequently published works. Detailed annotations accompany each item in the exhaustive list of secondary reviews and criticism. Fully superseded by Item 264, except for its prefatory printing of previously unpublished introductions by Hawkes.

262. Scotto, Robert M. *Three Contemporary Novelists: An Annotated Bibliography of Works by and about John Hawkes, Joseph Heller, and Thomas Pynchon*. Garland Reference Library of the Humanities 52. New York: Garland, 1977.

Enumerative, chronological record of American printings of works by Hawkes into 1976, followed by annotated coverage of major English-language commentary on him. Except for the introduction and Scotto's classified arrangement that enables convenient comparison with Heller and Pynchon, this volume is essentially superseded by Item 264.

263. Campbell, Lee G. "John Hawkes: A Bibliographical Checklist." *American Book Collector* ns 4.5 (September-October 1983): 48-54.

Abbreviated descriptive treatment of the American and British editions of Hawkes' separately published works, including books containing contributions by him. Chronologically ordered coverage extends into 1983, with informal notes about the printing histories of many individual volumes.

264. Hryciw-Wing, Carol A. *John Hawkes: A Research Guide*. Garland Reference Library of the Humanities 668. New York: Garland, 1986.

Updates and corrects the coverage of primary and secondary materials furnished by Item 261, nearly doubling the number of items listed. Otherwise, the format, style, and organization remain essentially identical.

HEINLEIN, ROBERT A. (1907-1988)

265. Panshin, Alexei. "Chronological Bibliography of Science Fiction by Robert Heinlein." In *Heinlein in Dimension: A Critical Analysis.* Chicago: Advent Publishers, 1966, 193-198.

   Enumerative treatment of primary texts into 1967. Superseded by Item 266, except for chronological arrangement.

266. Owings, Mark. *Robert A. Heinlein: A Bibliography.* Baltimore: Croatan House, 1973.

   A densely packed, quite informative, but rather unorthodox record of Heinlein's writings into 1972. Within an alphabetical arrangement, each enumerative entry traces first and subsequent printings of the item, including anthology appearances and foreign-language translations. Abbreviated descriptions register original price but little else.

267. Franklin, H. Bruce. "Checklist of Works by Robert A. Heinlein" and "Select List of Works about Robert A. Heinlein." In *Robert A. Heinlein: America as Science Fiction.* New York: Oxford Univ. Press, 1980, 214-223.

   Chronologically organized enumerative treatment of primary works and annotated coverage of selected secondary items into 1980. Though deliberately not exhaustive in its record of either works by or about Heinlein, nonetheless provides a useful updating of Item 266.

HELLER, JOSEPH (1923-)

268. Richwine, Keith N. *Joseph Heller and Catch-22: A Checklist.* Westminster, Md.: Catochin Press, 1972.

Pamphlet-length coverage of writings by and about Heller into 1971. Enumerative treatment of his separate publications includes their variant editions and accompanies lists of Heller's contributions to periodicals. Secondary section consists of unannotated record of reviews, including drama and film notices, along with separate listings of biographical pieces and general criticism. Fully superseded by subsequent bibliographical studies.

269. Weixlmann, Joseph. "A Bibliography of Joseph Heller's Catch-22." *Bulletin of Bibliography* 31.1 (January-March 1974): 32-37.

Unannotated checklist of secondary references into 1973, arranged alphabetically by author. Fully superseded by Item 271.

270. Scotto, Robert M. *Three Contemporary Novelists: An Annotated Bibliography of Works by and about John Hawkes, Joseph Heller, and Thomas Pynchon*. Garland Reference Library of the Humanities 52. New York: Garland, 1977.

Extensive but selective record of English-language writings by and about Heller into 1976. Both the enumerative coverage of primary items and the annotated treatment of secondary materials are organized by types of publications. Except for this arrangement and the easy comparisons it affords with the careers of Hawkes and Pynchon, Scotto's volume has been largely superseded by Item 271.

271. Keegan, Brenda M. *Joseph Heller: A Reference Guide*. Boston: G.K. Hall, 1978.

Enumerative checklist of Heller's published writings precedes an exhaustive, chronologically arranged record of reviews and critical articles on his work. All secondary entries accompanied by detailed contents notes. Coverage is for the period 1961-1977.

HENSLEY, JOE L. (1926-)

*272. "Bibliographie de Joe L. Hensley" and "Filmographie de Joe L. Hensley." *Les Durs à cuire* 4 (October 1982): 26-30, 31.

Item 2 cites this French crime fiction magazine by its English title, *Hard Boiled Dicks,* and indicates that this number featuring Hensley contains checklists of both his published writings and film work.

HERBERT, FRANK (1920-1986)

273. Levack, Daniel J. H. *Dune Master: A Frank Herbert Bibliography.* Meckler's Bibliographies on Science Fiction, Fantasy, and Horror 2. Westport, Ct.: Meckler, 1988.

Furnishes a detailed account of Herbert's work and a selected treatment of writings about him into early 1987. Primary coverage is presented in separate, alphabetically arranged sections for books and nonbook appearances. Books are accorded informal but thorough bibliographic descriptions, extending to variant editions and foreign-language translations. These physical descriptions are supplemented by photographic reproductions of dust jackets and paperback wrappers; each item is also accompanied by contents notes, often including a plot summary. Nonbook entries cover fiction and verse published in periodicals and anthologies as well as films, sound recordings, and some of Herbert's professional newspaper work. Excluded are letters, interviews, and his book reviews; also omitted are newspaper articles and foreign-language translations that escaped notice. Checklists for fiction, nonfiction, verse, and other media along with a chronology of Herbert's work provide alternate approaches to the materials. Secondary bibliography is representative.

HERSEY, JOHN (1914-)

274. Huse, Nancy Lyman. *John Hersey and James Agee: A Reference Guide*. Boston: G.K. Hall, 1978.

Brief checklist of works by Hersey precedes chronologically arranged, thoroughly annotated coverage of critical commentary on his work, into 1977. Scope is exhaustive, with only reviews confined to plot summary excluded.

HIMES, CHESTER (1909-1984)

275. Fabre, Michel. "Chester Himes' Published Works: A Tentative Checklist." *Black World* 21.5 (March 1972): 76-78.

Covers writings by and about Himes into 1972. Chronological, enumerative record of books includes the French editions of his novels and is followed by separate lists for the short stories and nonfiction pieces originally printed in magazines, in both English and French. Unannotated secondary section is restricted to more significant items and excludes reviews.

276. Hill, James Lee. "Bibliography of the Works of Chester Himes, Ann Petry and Frank Yerby." *Black Books Bulletin* 3.2 (Fall 1975): 60-72, esp. 61-65.

Enumerative, alphabetical listing of Himes' books supplemented by a record of the fiction and nonfiction he contributed to periodicals. Selected, annotated coverage of the critical literature, concluding with some reviews of Himes' books. References into 1972. Secondary coverage fuller and more extensive than that provided by Item 275.

HOCH, EDWARD D. (1930-)

277. Clark, William J., Edward D. Hoch, and Francis M. Nevins, Jr. "Edward D. Hoch: A Checklist." *Armchair Detective* 9.2 (February 1976): 102-111.

Thorough account of Hoch's writings into 1976. Divided into separate sections, beginning with enumerative coverage of books, story collections, and anthologies, followed by extensive listings of Hoch's short fiction and nonfiction, published under his own name and various bylines. Presentation of this large body of periodical literature is organized alphabetically by the magazine of original publication, then chronologically. Subsequent printings of these pieces in other periodicals or in collections is regularly noted. Film and television adaptations of Hoch's work are also described. Item 2 reports that the authors revised and privately printed a new edition of this bibliography in 1979.

IRVING, JOHN (1942-)

278. Reilly, Edward C. "A John Irving Bibliography." *Bulletin of Bibliography* 42.1 (March 1985): 12-18.

Thorough coverage of published writings by and about Irving from 1965 through 1983. Enumerative primary record is arranged chronologically within type of publication. Unannotated secondary treatment seeks to be comprehensive for longer critical commentary but is deliberately selective for reviews.

JACKSON, CHARLES (1903-1968)

279. Leonard, Shirley. "Charles Reginald Jackson: A Checklist." *Bulletin of Bibliography* 28.4 (October-December 1971): 137-141.

Furnishes sound coverage of primary works into 1969, with separate sections for Jackson's books, including foreign-language translations, collections of short stories, and his contributions of both fiction and nonfiction to periodicals. Enumerative treatment of the novels details many variant editions.

280. ----------. "Charles Reginald Jackson: A Critical Checklist." *Serif* 10.3 (Fall 1973): 32-40.

Complements Item 279, providing a two-part presentation of secondary materials. The first section lists and generously annotates reviews of Jackson's books published in major periodicals; the second section summarizes bio-critical pieces on him, excluding obituaries. Citations as late as 1967.

JACKSON, SHIRLEY (1919-1965)

281. Phillips, Robert S. "Shirley Jackson: A Checklist." *Papers of the Bibliographical Society of America* 56.1 (January-March 1962): 110-113.

Chronological coverage of primary sources into 1960. Emphasis of this enumerative listing of Jackson's writings is on first printings, with anthologizations and foreign-language editions excluded. Compiled with the writer's assistance, the bibliography identifies many of her humor pieces that appeared in popular magazines.

282. ----------. "Shirley Jackson: A Chronology and Supplementary Checklist." *Papers of the Bibliographical Society of America* 60.2 (April-June 1966): 203-213.

Records works omitted from Item 281 and updates its chronological primary coverage through 1965. Unannotated account of secondary materials is divided among general criticism, biographical pieces, and reviews of Jackson's books published in national magazines and newspapers.

JONES, GAYL (1949-)

283. Weixlmann, Joe. "A Gayl Jones Bibliography." *Callaloo* 7.1 [also cited as No. 20] (Winter 1984): 119-131.

Exemplary coverage of writings by and about Jones into 1983. Chronological, enumerative lists of primary materials include foreign-language translations of the novels, detailed record of periodical contributions, and the printing histories of individual poems and stories. Unannotated record of critical commentary notes items appearing in unindexed black American journals and other bibliographically marginalized publications.

JONES, JAMES (1921-1977)

284. Hopkins, John R. *James Jones: A Checklist*. Detroit: Bruccoli Clark/Gale, 1974.

Chronological account of Jones' published writings into 1974. Section devoted to books supplements its abbreviated physical description of first editions with photographs of title pages and an enumerative list of subsequent issues, excluding foreign-language translations. Record of periodicals notes later reprintings.

JONES, MADISON (1925-)

285. Gretlund, Jan Nordby. "Madison Jones: A Bibliography." *Bulletin of Bibliography* 39.3 (September 1982): 117-120.

Thorough accounting of published writings by and about Jones into 1982. Chronological, enumerative record of primary materials includes the translations of his books into foreign languages as well as collected and republished periodical pieces. Unannotated secondary list is arranged alphabetically.

KEENE, DAY (d. 1969)

*286. Schleret, Jean-Jacques, Jean-François Naudon, and Jean-Paul Schweig. "Day Keene: Bibliographie." *Amis du crime* 10 (October 1981): 31-48.

Item 2 reports that this number of the French journal of crime fiction contains a chronological checklist of Keene's works. The books section records American, British, and French editions and carries plot summaries for his novels. The selected record of secondary sources emphasizes references in books.

KEROUAC, JACK (1922-1969)

287. Charters, Ann. *A Bibliography of Works by Jack Kerouac (Jean Louis Lebris De Kerouac) 1939-1967*. New York: Phoenix Book Shop, 1967. Rev.ed. New York: Phoenix Book Shop, 1975.

Provides a detailed inventory of works by Kerouac into 1975. Arranged by publication format, with individual sections for separate publications (including broadsides), contributions to periodicals, translations of his works, recordings, musical settings, and interviews (extending to articles with quotations). Full descriptive treatment of books and their variant editions, with entries supplemented by notes that explain the circumstances of composition and publication. Thorough indexing allows the tracing of pieces first printed in periodicals. Secondary literature excluded.

288. Le Pellec, Yves. "Jack Kerouac and the American Critics: A Selected Bibliography." *Caliban* [Univ. de Toulouse-Le Mirail] 9 (1973): 77-92.

Offers a highly selective list of secondary items published during the 1950s and 1960s. Deliberately chosen to provide a cross-section of critical response to Kerouac during this period, all entries are accompanied by extensive analytical notes. These carefully prepared annotations assure the continued usefulness of this checklist, whose bibliographic information has long since been superseded.

289. Gargan, William. "Jack Kerouac: Biography and Criticism--A Working Bibliography." *Moody Street Irregulars* 6-7 (Winter-Spring 1980): 21-23.

Unannotated inventory of secondary references into 1979, including numerous citations to little magazines and foreign-language publications.

290. Bierkins, Jef. "Supplement to William Gargan's 'Jack Kerouac: Biography and Criticism--A Working Bibliography': Works in

the Dutch Language." *Moody Street Irregulars* 8 (Summer-Fall 1980): 18.

Supplements Item 289, recording Dutch responses to Kerouac published from 1963 through 1979.

291. Nisonger, Thomas Evans. "Jack Kerouac: A Bibliography of Biographical and Critical Material, 1950--1979." *Bulletin of Bibliography* 37.1 (January-March 1980): 23-32.

Unannotated coverage of secondary sources through 1979. Arranged by type of commentary, with separate sections for articles, books, reviews, and other formats. Scope not as extensive as Item 292 but lists numerous items omitted by Milewski.

292. Milewski, Robert J. *Jack Kerouac: An Annotated Bibliography of Secondary Sources, 1944-1979.* Scarecrow Author Bibliographies 52. Metuchen, N.J.: Scarecrow Press, 1981.

Broad but uneven account of secondary references through 1979. Organized by the criticism's published format, with an index that allows alternative approaches to the material. Notes accompanying most entries summarize the themes, or argument of the item.

293. Poteet, Maurice. "A Select Québec-France Bibliographie sur Kerouac." *Moody Street Irregulars* 11 (Spring-Summer 1982): 7-9.

Lists and briefly annotates in English French-language commentary on Kerouac from 1963 to 1980.

KESEY, KEN (1935-)

294. Weixlmann, Joseph. "Ken Kesey: A Bibliography." *Western American Literature* 10.3 (Fall 1975): 219-231.

Enumerative primary and unannotated secondary checklist of published Kesey materials into 1975. Thorough coverage of writings by Kesey includes numerous references to his contributions to countercultural publications. Record of critical commentary about his work focuses on more nationally prominent journals, and Weixlmann suggests some underground and other bibliographically fugitive items may have been omitted.

KING, STEPHEN (1947-)

295. Ketchum, Marty, Daniel J.H. Levack, and Jeff Levin. "Stephen King: A Bibliography." In *Fear Itself: The Horror Fiction of Stephen King*. Ed. Tim Underwood and Chuck Miller. San Francisco and Columbia, Pa.: Underwood-Miller, 1982, 231-246.

Limited to first appearances, with entries for fiction and nonfiction in books and non-book formats. Also includes listings for interviews and secondary references. Remains valuable for its descriptive information regarding King's separate publications.

296. Leonard, Stephanie. "Stephen King Bibliography." *Castle Rock: The Stephen King Newsletter* June 1985: 6-7; July 1985: 4, 7.

Account of works by and about King prepared under his auspices.

297. Collings, Michael R. *The Annotated Guide to Stephen King: A Primary and Secondary Bibliography of the Works of America's Premier Horror Writer*. Starmont Reference Guide 8. Mercer Island, Wash.: Starmont House, 1986.

Primary coverage includes separate alphabetically arranged sections for King's book-length fiction, collections of his fiction, short fiction and poetry in periodicals, his nonfiction, criticism, and reviews, and audio-visual treatments of his works. Annotations, provided for all entries, summarize plot and indicate theme. Though the alphabetical listings of secondary materials are selective, their scope is extensive, recording and carefully annotating nearly 600 book-length studies, articles, and reviews.

Emphasis is on English-language materials, with citations into 1986. Builds on and incorporates information from Items 295, 296, and 298.

298. ----------. "Checklist of Works by and about Stephen King." In *The Many Facets of Stephen King*. Starmont Studies in Literary Criticism 11. San Bernardino, Calif.: Borgo Press, 1986, c.1985, 142-181.

Enumerative primary coverage includes separate sections for books, short fiction and poetry, nonfiction, and interviews as well as one for filmed versions of King's work. Unannotated record of secondary sources is selective but extensive, including numerous reviews from local newspapers. Organization throughout is alphabetical, with references into 1985.

299. ----------, and David Engebretson. *The Shorter Works of Stephen King*. Starmont Studies in Literary Criticism 9. San Bernardino, Calif.: Borgo Press, 1986, c.1985.

Alphabetical checklist of King's short fiction and poetry (pp. 187-193) preceded by chronologically arranged synopses of each story, with coverage into 1985.

300. Collings, Michael R. "Filmography." In *The Films of Stephen King*. Starmont Studies in Literary Criticism 12. San Bernardino, Calif.: Borgo Press, 1987, c.1986, 167-188.

Alphabetically arranged record of production and credits information about filmed versions of King's fiction, including non-commercial productions, into 1985. More detailed than analogous section in Items 297 and 298.

301. ----------. "Beginnings: 'King's Garbage Truck'" and "Some Notes on Foreign Publications." In *The Stephen King Phenomenon*. Starmont Studies in Literary Criticism 14. San Bernardino, Calif.: Borgo Press, 1987, 107-123, 125-133.

These chapters furnish specialized bibliographic information on King's regular columns for his college's weekly newspaper and about European editions and translations of his work. References extend into 1986.

KNIGHT, DAMON (1922-)

302. Miranda, Vincent. "Damon Knight: Bibliography." *Magazine of Fantasy and Science Fiction* 51.5 (November 1976): 26-28.

     Highly condensed but nevertheless informative checklist of works by Knight into 1976. Individual lists for stories, collections, novels, his editorial work, and his translations, each arranged chronologically. No secondary coverage.

KOSINSKI, JERZY (1933-)

303. Rusch, Frederic E. "Jerzy Kosinski: A Checklist." *Bulletin of Bibliography* 31.1 (January-March 1974): 6-9.

     Alphabetically organized, primary and secondary coverage through early 1973. Enumerative treatment of books by Kosinski complemented by listing of his periodical contributions. Record of general commentary and reviews is unannotated. Largely redundant with Item 304 but includes references both by and about Kosinski not entered by Walsh and Northouse.

304. Walsh, Thomas P., and Cameron Northouse. *John Barth, Jerzy Kosinski, and Thomas Pynchon: A Reference Guide.* Boston: G.K. Hall, 1977.

     Enumerative checklist of primary publications precedes annotated chronological account of secondary materials through 1973.

305. Klinkowitz, Jerome, and Daniel J. Cahill. "The Great Jerzy Kosinski Press War: A Bibliography." *Missouri Review* 6.3 (Summer 1983): 171-175.

Chronologically arranged, annotated checklist of secondary commentary published in the American popular and regional press on Kosinski, principally during 1982 and reflecting controversy about the accuracy of his autobiographical statements and the legitimacy of his authorship.

LAFFERTY, R. A. (1914-)

306. Drumm, Chris. *An R.A. Lafferty Checklist: A Bibliographical Chronology*. Polk City, Iowa: Chris Drumm, 1983. Rev. ed. in preparation, San Bernardino, Calif.: Borgo Press.

Chronological account of Lafferty's works into 1983. Enumerative treatment of books registers first as well as subsequent editions and translations, furnishing for most of them total pagination and prices at original publication. Handling of short stories and other contributions to periodicals notes many of the numerous reprintings in both Lafferty's own collections and in multi-author anthologies.

LE GUIN, URSULA K. (1929-)

307. Levin, Jeff. "Ursula K. Le Guin: A Select Bibliography." *Science-Fiction Studies* 2.3 (November 1975): 204-208.

Provides a thorough record of Le Guin's prose fiction through 1974 and a selected list of her nonfiction work. Chronologically ordered, enumerative treatment notes subsequent reprintings as well as foreign editions. Bibliographic data incorporated in Item 309.

308. Bittner, James W. "A Survey of Le Guin Criticism." In *Ursula K. Le Guin: Voyager to Inner Lands and Outer Space*. Ed. Joe De Bolt. Port Washington, N.Y.: Kennikat Press, 1979, 31-49, 200-204.

A discursive account of the principal critical discussions of Le Guin into 1977, which carefully evaluates and analyzes selected items. Organization is generally chronological. Annotations of individual articles remain valuable.

309. Levin, Jeff. "Bibliographic Checklist of the Works of Ursula K. Le Guin." In *The Language of the Night*. Ed. Susan Wood. New York: Putnam, 1979, 237-270.

Detailed enumerative record of Le Guin's published writings to October 1978, except her poetry and quotations used in book jacket blurbs and other advertisements. The basic bibliographic information is incorporated in Item 312, but Levin's coverage of minor items and his account of variant editions, especially foreign-language translations, remain unique as does his alphabetical arrangement within different categories of Le Guin's writings. Also distinct is the concluding section of secondary items that includes original quotations from Le Guin.

310. Tymn, Marshall B. "A Bibliography." In *Ursula K. Le Guin*. Ed. Joseph D. Olander and Martin Harry Greenberg. New York: Taplinger, 1979, 241-246.

Primary and secondary record, with strongest coverage for pre-1976 period. Treatment of works by Le Guin is arranged by types of work, with separate sections for her books and pamphlets, short fiction, and her articles and essays. List of critical commentary is deliberately selective. Bibliographical information fully incorporated in Item 312.

311. Levin, Jeff, and Jim Bittner. "Of the Open Hills: A Poetic Bibliography of Ursula K. Le Guin." *Anthology of Speculative Poetry* 4 (1980): 4-5.

Chronological checklist of Le Guin's poetry to 1979. Information incorporated in Item 312.

312. Cogell, Elizabeth Cummins. *Ursula K. Le Guin: A Primary and Secondary Bibliography*. Boston: G.K. Hall, 1983.

Comprehensive chronological record of English-language publications by and about Le Guin through 1979 and into 1980. Enumerative primary coverage, divided among fiction, nonfiction, and miscellaneous media, carefully notes multiple appearances of pieces, including anthology reprintings. Secondary bibliography excludes insubstantial reviews but thoroughly annotates all entries in its otherwise extensive scope.

LEIBER, FRITZ (1910-)

313. Lewis, Al. "Fritz Leiber: A Bibliography." *Magazine of Fantasy and Science Fiction* 37.1 (July 1969): 63-68.

Enumerative, unannotated checklist of primary published materials into 1969. Chronological arrangement with separate sections for Leiber's books, stories, and nonfiction articles. First publication only is recorded.

314. Morgan, Chris. *Fritz Leiber: A Bibliography 1934-1979*. Birmingham, Eng.: Morgenstern, 1979.

Conscientious record into 1979 of works by Leiber, including separate, chronological sections for his books, nonfiction articles, and short stories. Partially descriptive treatment of books lists first printing and all other known American and British editions, frequently noting their price, print run, and jacket illustrator. Inventory of articles excludes only minor fanzine items.

315. Frane, Jeff, and Roger C. Schlobin. "Primary Bibliography" and "Annotated Secondary Bibliography." In Frane, *Fritz Leiber*. Starmont Reader's Guides to Contemporary Science Fiction and Fantasy Authors 8. Mercer Island, Wash.: Starmont House, 1980, 48-62.

Alphabetical, annotated list of Leiber's books, specifying and briefly describing contents, followed by an annotated record of major critical pieces on his work. Citations extend into late 1979.

316. Staicar, Tom. "Bibliography." In *Fritz Leiber*. New York: Ungar, 1983, 128-131.

> Selected primary and secondary coverage with references as late as 1981. The checklist's value lies in this currency, updating the coverage of Items 314 and 315.

LUTZ, JOHN (1939-)

317. Nevins, Francis M., Jr. "Checklist of the Short Stories of John Lutz." *Poisoned Pen* 1.3 (May 1978): 13-15. Revised and reprinted in *Armchair Detective* 12.3 (Summer 1979): 278-279.

> Presents Lutz's stories chronologically according to the periodicals within which they originally appeared. Citations into 1979.

MACDONALD, JOHN D. (1916-1986)

318. Moffatt, Len, June G. Moffatt, and William J. Clark. *The JDM Master Checklist: A Bibliography of the Published Writings of John D. MacDonald*. Downey, Calif.: Moffatt House, 1969.

> First effort at a comprehensive primary bibliography, this annotated checklist covers MacDonald's books as well as contributions to periodicals, with extensive information on foreign editions and cross references for pseudonyms. Bibliographic information largely incorporated in Item 319.

319. Shine, Walter, and Jean Shine. *A Bibliography of the Published Works of John D. MacDonald*. Gainesville: Patrons of the Libraries, Univ. of Florida, 1980.

> Very informative but eccentrically organized account of writings by and about MacDonald through most of 1980. Enumerative primary sections provide publishing histories of American and British editions; they also furnish considerable detail about periodical fiction (arranged by magazine), nonfiction articles

(listed by type of essay), and foreign-language translations. Secondary coverage is unannotated.

MACDONALD, ROSS (1915-1983)

320. Bruccoli, Matthew J. *Kenneth Millar/Ross Macdonald: A Checklist.* Detroit: Bruccoli Clark/Gale, 1971.

Record of published writings by Millar under his own name and the pseudonym Ross Macdonald into 1971, chronologically arranged within published format. Abbreviated descriptive handling of books is supplemented by photographic reproductions of title pages. Coverage of nonbook items extends to marginal and ephemeral materials. All bibliographic information fully incorporated in Item 321.

321. ----------. *Ross Macdonald/Kenneth Millar: A Descriptive Bibliography.* Pittsburgh: Univ. of Pittsburgh Press, 1983.

Definitive treatment of Millar's published writings as both Millar and Macdonald, into 1981. Full bibliographic description of books supplemented by photographic reproductions of title pages and covers. A separate section records his blurbs for other writers' books.

322. Skinner, Robert F. *The Hard-Boiled Explicator: A Guide to the Study of Dashiell Hammett, Raymond Chandler and Ross Macdonald.* Metuchen, N.J.: Scarecrow Press, 1985.

Furnishes comprehensive coverage of the secondary literature about Macdonald into 1984. Arranged in four sections: articles and essays, books and monographs, fugitive materials, and book reviews, with items for all the writers treated included in each section. Consequently, the index must be used to locate citations specific to Macdonald. Most entries fully annotated.

MADDEN, DAVID (1933-)

323. Perrault, Anna H. "A David Madden Bibliography: 1952-1981." *Bulletin of Bibliography* 39.3 (September 1982): 104-116.

> Thorough checklist of published writings by and about Madden through 1981. Primary works are presented chronologically within their respective genres. Enumerative treatment of the novels and collected stories is followed by separate sections for short fiction, poetry, plays and dramatic pieces, books of criticism, nonfiction articles, and Madden's own reviews. Reviews of Madden's books are listed without annotation immediately after the primary entry; the secondary sections proper focus on critical articles, biographical notices, and interviews.

MAILER, NORMAN (1923-)

324. Sokoloff, B.A. *A Bibliography of Norman Mailer*. Darby, Pa.: Darby Books, 1969. Rpt. Norwood, Pa.: Norwood Editions, 1973; Folcroft, Pa.: Folcroft Library Editions, 1974.

> Primary and secondary coverage into 1969. Enumerative record of Mailer's published works includes information about editions of his books subsequent to the first, which remains useful; otherwise, Sokoloff's account has been essentially superseded by Item 329.

325. Adams, Laura. "Criticism of Norman Mailer: A Selected Checklist." *Modern Fiction Studies* 17.3 (Autumn 1971): 455-463.

> Unannotated record of criticism arranged according to Mailer's individual books, with an introductory section for general commentary. Bibliographic information fully incorporated in Item 329.

326. Lucid, Robert F. "A Checklist of Mailer's Published Work." In *Norman Mailer: The Man and His Work*. Boston: Little, Brown, 1971, 299-310.

> Chronological record of Mailer's book and periodical contributions from 1941 to 1970. Includes references to less prominent journals and notes republications of items. Bibliographical information essentially covered in Item 329.

327. Shepard, Douglas H. "Norman Mailer: A Preliminary Bibliography of Secondary Comment, 1948-1968." *Bulletin of Bibliography* 29.2 (April-June 1972): 37-45.

> Tentative but substantial checklist of criticism and reviews. Alphabetical arrangement, with strictly biographical items omitted. Largely superseded by Item 329.

*328. Sadoya, Shigenobu. "A Bibliography of Norman Mailer." *Studies of American Novels* 1 (25 May 1973).

> Item 329 reports that this Japanese journal article includes a section on Mailer's work and reception in Japan.

329. Adams, Laura. *Norman Mailer: A Comprehensive Bibliography*. Scarecrow Author Bibliographies 20. Metuchen, N.J.: Scarecrow Press, 1974.

> Sound list of materials by and about Mailer through 1973. Enumerative primary sections record unpublished manuscripts of completed works and duly note subsequent publication of periodical pieces but exclude works published outside the United States. Coverage of secondary reviews and commentary is extensive, though not annotated.

MAJOR, CLARENCE (1936-)

330. Weixlmann, Joe. "Clarence Major: A Checklist of Criticism." *Obsidian* 4.2 (1978): 101-113.

Thorough but unannotated record of secondary literature on Major through 1976. Coverage of reviews is organized by genre, with separate sections for notices of novels, nonfiction, the anthologies Major has edited, and his books of poetry. Other sections list biographical articles, criticism, and pieces containing his printed remarks. Scope extends to many unindexed counter-cultural, Afro-American, and related little magazines.

331. ----------, and Clarence Major. "Towards a Primary Bibliography of Clarence Major." *Black American Literature Forum* 13.2 (Summer 1979): 70-72.

Detailed inventory of Major's published writings into 1979. Enumerative presentation of books.

MALAMUD, BERNARD (1914-1986)

332. Kosofsky, Rita Nathalie. *Bernard Malamud: An Annotated Checklist*. Serif Series 7. Kent, Ohio: Kent State Univ. Press, 1969.

Records American and British publications by and about Malamud through 1968. Enumerative treatment of books; other primary coverage includes detailed documentation of the original appearances of stories and their subsequent reprintings in collections and anthologies. Classified and annotated secondary sections list reviews separately from other criticism. Though Item 337 supersedes Kosofsky's secondary treatment, her documentation of primary sources remains valuable.

333. Sher, Morris. *Bernard Malamud: A Partially Annotated Bibliography*. Johannesburg: Univ. of Witwatersrand, Dept. of Bibliography, Librarianship, and Typography, 1970.

Checklist of primary and secondary texts into 1969. Enumerative treatment of Malamud's novels includes a record of foreign-language translations, a feature updated and superseded by Item 336. Secondary coverage annotates critical articles only and is essentially superseded by Item 337.

334. Risty, Donald. "A Comprehensive Checklist of Malamud Criticism." In *The Fiction of Bernard Malamud*. Ed. Richard Astro and Jackson J. Benson. Corvallis: Oregon State Univ. Press, 1977, 163-190.

Thorough but unannotated secondary coverage into 1975. Alphabetical arrangement within a scheme classified by the format of critical commentary. Largely superseded by Item 337.

335. Habich, Robert D. "Bernard Malamud: A Bibliographical Survey." *Studies in American Jewish Literature* 4.1 (Spring 1978): 78-84.

Discursive account of Malamud's critical reception and an evaluation of the state of scholarship on the novelist. Though Habich's bibliographic information has been fully incorporated in subsequent publications, his annotations remain valuable.

336. Grau, Joseph A. "Bernard Malamud: A Bibliographical Addendum." *Bulletin of Bibliography* 37.4 (October-December 1980): 157-166, 184; "Bernard Malamud: A Further Bibliographical Addendum." *Bulletin of Bibliography* 38.2 (April-June 1981): 101-104.

Deliberately designed to supplement the primary and secondary coverage of Items 332 and 334. Enumerative treatment of works by Malamud provides detailed record of translations and also traces the publishing history of periodical contributions. Though secondary checklist has been superseded by Item 337, Grau's account of primary items remains valuable.

337. Salzberg, Joel. *Bernard Malamud: A Reference Guide*. Boston: G.K. Hall, 1985.

Well annotated record of critical commentary on Malamud through 1983. Comprehensive coverage, except for selective treatment of brief reviews in regional newspapers and representative handling of foreign-language references. Well indexed.

MANFRED, FREDERICK (1912-)

338. Kellogg, George. *Frederick Manfred: A Bibliography*. Swallow Pamphlets 17. Denver: Alan Swallow, 1965.

Thorough account through 1964 of works by and about Manfred, whose usual byline is Feike Feikema. Separate sections for his books, his contributions to periodicals (including poems, nonfiction, and short stories), and writings about him (subdivided between general commentary and reviews of specific novels). All sections are alphabetically organized, with the enumerative treatment of his books recording variant editions as well as foreign-language translations and the unannotated secondary coverage extending not only to unpublished doctoral dissertations but also reviews in regional newspapers.

MATHEWS, HARRY (1930-)

339. [Winkfield, Trevor]. "Harry Mathews: A Bibliography." *Juillard* (Winter 1968-1969, Pinecone Supplement): [12-13].

Enumerative record of primary works to 1968. Fully superseded by Item 340.

340. McPheron, William. "Harry Mathews: A Checklist." *Review of Contemporary Fiction* 7.3 (Fall 1987): 197-226.

Exhaustive enumerative treatment of works by Mathews and detailed, unannotated record of critical commentary about him, through October 1986. Primary coverage includes foreign-language versions of his novels as well as their European reviews; reprintings of periodical contributions are also carefully recorded. Checklist prefaced by analysis of critical reactions to Mathews's work.

MATTHIESSEN, PETER (1927-)

341. Nicholas, D. *Peter Matthiessen, A Bibliography: 1951-1979*. Canoga Park, Calif.: Oriana Press, 1979.

Sound coverage of writings by and about Matthiessen through 1979. Informally descriptive treatment of Matthiessen's books is supplemented by reproductions of many title pages. Brief contents notes accompany primary references, but secondary sections are wholly unannotated though thorough, except for omission of local newspaper reviews.

342. [Young, James Dean]. "A Peter Matthiessen Checklist." *Critique* 21.2 (1979): 30-38.

Thorough record of primary and secondary writings into 1979. Enumerative treatment of works by Matthiessen covers variant editions of books, including an exacting account of foreign-language translations, as well as tracing reprintings of periodical pieces. Secondary coverage is sound but not annotated. Largely redundant with Item 341, but both contain information lacking in the other and consequently complement one another.

MAY, JULIAN (1931-)

343. Dikty, Thaddeus, and R. Reginald. *The Work of Julian May: An Annotated Bibliography and Guide.* Bibliographies of Modern Authors 3. San Bernardino, Calif.: Borgo Press, 1985.

Exhaustive presentation of works by and writings about May, with references into 1985. Arranged by type of publication, with separate sections for books, articles, and short fiction as well as such educational formats as study prints and lesson plans. The vast majority of this bibliography is occupied by references to May's many juvenile nonfiction books and her related articles and encyclopedia pieces, so that citations to her science fiction constitute only a small part of the volume.

MCALLISTER, BRUCE (1946-)

344. Bourquin, David Ray. *The Work of Bruce McAllister: An Annotated Bibliography and Guide.* Bibliographies of Modern Authors 10. San Bernardino, Calif.: Borgo Press, 1985.

Furnishes an account both of the writings and editorial work by McAllister and of commentary on him through late 1985. Primary coverage divided into categories, with enumerative treatment of his books, chronological presentation of periodical contributions, including indications of their reprinting histories, separate checklists for McAllister's nonfiction and poetry, and a record of his editorial posts. Handling of secondary sources extends to reviews but is unannotated.

MCBAIN, ED (1926-)

*345. Naudon, Jean-François. "Bibliographie de Evan Hunter et compagnie." *Polar* 9 (February 1980): 11-17.

According to Item 2, a chronological checklist of English and American editions and their French translations.

MCCAFFREY, ANNE (1926-)

346. Arbur, Rosemarie. *Leigh Brackett, Marion Zimmer Bradley, Anne McCaffrey: A Primary and Secondary Bibliography*. Boston: G.K. Hall, 1982.

Provides an enumerative checklist of published writings by and about McCaffrey into 1980. Materials treated include McCaffrey's fiction, nonfiction, and nonprint appearances, as well as reviews, articles, and essays about her works. Consistently lengthy annotations for secondary sources describe tone, argument, and scope of each item.

MCCARTHY, MARY (1912-)

347. Goldman, Sherli Evens. *Mary McCarthy: A Bibliography*. New York: Harcourt, Brace and World, 1968.

Scrupulously thorough, fully descriptive account of primary materials through 1967, with separate, chronologically ordered sections for books, contributions to books, contributions to periodicals, and miscellaneous items. Another section for translations of McCarthy's works is organized by foreign language and is the only one for which bibliographical information is less than exemplary.

348. Schweyer, Janine. "L'Oeuvre de Mary McCarthy devant la critique: Première bibliographie des livres, articles et recensions parus jusqu'en 1970." *Recherches Anglaises et Américaines* 4 (1971): 170-197.

Extremely thorough record of American and British secondary materials through 1970. Alphabetically arranged by author or, if item is unsigned, by serial publication, the unannotated list includes items from many local newspapers and small magazines.

MCCULLERS, CARSON (1917-1967)

349. Stewart, Stanley. "Carson McCullers, 1940-1956: A Selected Checklist." *Bulletin of Bibliography* 22.8 (January-April 1959): 182-185.

Furnishes a working core of primary and secondary references. Record of works by McCullers excludes foreign-language translations and focuses on contributions to indexed periodicals. List of critical commentary is restricted to English-language items and excludes some categories of reviews. Basic bibliographic information fully incorporated in subsequent book-length bibliographies of McCullers.

350. Phillips, Robert S. "Carson McCullers, 1956-1964: A Selected Checklist." *Bulletin of Bibliography* 24.5 (September-December 1964): 113-116.

Designed to supplement and update Item 348. Offers similar format and depth of coverage but extends scope to such categories as biographical sketches, recordings, and parodies. Bibliographic information fully covered by later book-length bibliographies of McCullers.

351. Stanley, William T. "Carson McCullers: 1965-1969, A Selected Checklist." *Bulletin of Bibliography* 27.4 (October-December 1970): 91-93.

   Continues treatment of Items 349 and 350, with similar format and scope; also superseded by later book-length works.

352. Dorsey, James E. "Carson McCullers and Flannery O'Connor: A Checklist of Graduate Research." *Bulletin of Bibliography* 32.4 (October-December 1975): 162-164.

   Supplements Items 349, 350, and 351 by comprehensively listing masters theses and doctoral dissertations submitted through 1974. Arrangement is alphabetical by author, with no annotations.

353. Kiernan, Robert F. *Katherine Anne Porter and Carson McCullers: A Reference Guide*. Boston: G.K. Hall, 1976, 95-169, 185-194.

   Chronologically ordered record of critical commentary on McCullers through 1973, with some references as late as 1974-75. All entries are carefully annotated and thoroughly indexed. Though its bibliographical information is largely superseded by Item 355, Kiernan's chronological arrangement and annotations remain useful.

354. Shapiro, Adrian Michael. "Carson McCullers: A Descriptive Bibliography." Diss. Indiana Univ. 1977.

   A model descriptive inventory of McCullers' work, with separate, chronologically organized sections for her books, contributions to books, contributions to periodicals, interviews, and miscellaneous items. Revised and incorporated in Item 355.

355. Shapiro, Adrian M., Jackson R. Bryer, and Kathleen Field. *Carson McCullers: A Descriptive Listing and Annotated Bibliography of Criticism*. Garland Reference Library of the Humanities 142. New York: Garland, 1981.

Exhaustive coverage into 1978 of writings by and about McCullers in English. Primary treatment offers full descriptive accounts of the American and British editions of her novels; also traced in comparable detail are her contributions to books, pamphlets, magazines, and newspapers. Secondary record is arranged alphabetically by type of publication, with separate sections for books, periodical articles, and reviews about her. The list of reviews is distinguished by extensive inclusion of local newspaper notices. All secondary references are accompanied by thorough contents notes. Foreign-language editions of McCullers' work as well as their reception in non-English language countries are excluded.

356. Bixby, George. "Carson McCullers: A Bibliographical Checklist." *American Book Collector* ns 5.1 (January-February 1984): 38-43.

Brief descriptive accounts of McCullers' separate publications as well as of the books to which she contributed, with latest reference to a 1979 item. Supplemental notes recounting publishing and production details enhance entries for many titles.

MCGUANE, THOMAS (1939-)

357. McCaffery, Larry. "Thomas McGuane: A Bibliography, 1969-1978." *Bulletin of Bibliography* 35.4 (October-December 1978): 169-171.

Enumerative checklist of works by McGuane extends to his nonfiction sports articles and screenplays. Unannotated secondary record includes interviews as well as reviews of books and relevant films. Coverage into 1978.

MCMURTRY, LARRY (1936-)

358. Peavy, Charles D. "A Larry McMurtry Bibliography." *Western American Literature* 3.3 (Fall 1968): 235-248.

Highly detailed, enumerative coverage of writings by McMurtry through 1967. Separate chronological lists for his fiction, poetry, and nonfiction; a thorough record, arranged alphabetically by author, of McMurtry's numerous book reviews for the *Houston Post*, and a careful census of both published and unpublished manuscript holdings in the University of Houston Library. No secondary items cited.

359. ----------. "Selected Bibliography." In *Larry McMurtry*. Twayne's United States Author Series 291. Boston: Twayne, 1977, 127-141.

Following the format of Item 358, updates primary record into 1976, including an extensive list of book reviews McMurtry wrote for the *Washington Post* and a section on his film criticism. Very selective but well annotated list of secondary sources follows primary coverage.

360. Huber, Dwight. "Larry McMurtry: A Selected Bibliography." In *Larry McMurtry--Unredeemed Dreams: A Collection of Bibliography, Essays, and Interview*. Ed. Dorey Schmidt. Living Author Series 1. Edinburg, Texas: School of Humanities, Pan American Univ., 1978, 59-69. 2nd ed. 1981, 52-61.

Selective coverage of primary and secondary references into 1977. Occasionally serves to update the record of McMurtry's writings provided by Item 359 but is most valuable for its unannotated list of commentary on him, with separate sections for reviews of books, reviews of screenplays, unpublished graduate research, and biographical sources as well as general criticism.

MCPHERSON, JAMES ALAN (1943-)

361. Fikes, Robert, Jr. "The Works of an 'American' Writer: A James A. McPherson Bibliography." *College Language Association Journal* 22.4 (June 1979): 415-423.

Sound record of writings by and about McPherson for the period 1968 through 1978. Chronologically organized, enumerative primary coverage extends to reprintings of periodical contributions in anthologies and other collected works. Unannotated lists of reviews and general criticism focus on nationally prominent journals.

METCALF, PAUL (1917-)

362. Gildzen, Alex. "Paul Metcalf: A Checklist." *Credences* 8-9 [also cited as 3.3-4] (March 1980): 39-52.

Furnishes a thorough account of writings by and about Metcalf through 1979. Primary coverage is arranged chronologically within individual sections for Metcalf's separate publications-- including books, pamphlets, and broadsides--his contributions to books, contributions to periodicals, and miscellaneous items. Treatment of books is informally descriptive, specifying variant editions as well as other data about publishing history; scope of periodical references is very broad, including many little magazines. Secondary section is unannotated.

MILLAR, MARGARET (1915-)

363. Lachman, Marvin. "Margaret Millar: The Checklist of an 'Unknown' Mystery Writer." *Armchair Detective* 3.1 (1969-1970): 85-88.

Chronological, annotated record of Millar's novels through 1968. Variant editions briefly recorded, but emphasis is on the notes, which summarize plot and indicate critical response.

MORRIS, WRIGHT (1910-)

364. Linden, Stanton J., and David Madden. "A Wright Morris Bibliography." *Critique* 4.3 (Winter 1961-1962): 77-87.

Thorough checklist of writings by and about Morris, with references into early 1962. Chronological presentation of primary materials is arranged in separate sections for Morris' books and the reviews of them, short stories originally published in magazines, his text-photography, and finally his non-fiction articles and reviews. Treatment of books is enumerative but records variant editions and translations; subsequent reprintings of periodical contributions are carefully noted. Secondary sections for biography and for general criticism are unannotated but reasonably comprehensive.

365. Boyce, Robert L. "A Wright Morris Bibliography." In *Conversations with Wright Morris: Critical Views and Responses*. Ed. Robert E. Knoll. Lincoln: Univ. of Nebraska Press, 1977, 169-206.

Adopts the arrangement of Item 364, incorporating its information, and extending Linden and Madden's coverage through 1975. Comparable level of scrupulous detail in the treatment of primary references. Secondary sources are also organized chronologically and listed without annotation.

366. Crump, G.B. "Bibliography." In *The Novels of Wright Morris: A Critical Interpretation*. Lincoln: Univ. of Nebraska Press, 1978, 243-248.

Essentially a selective version of Item 365, but deliberately arranged alphabetically in order to provide a different approach to the bibliographic citations.

MORRISON, TONI (1931-)

367. Fikes, Robert, Jr. "Echoes from Small Town Ohio: A Toni Morrison Bibliography." *Obsidian* 5.1-2 (1980): 142-148.

Thorough coverage of writings by and about Morrison into 1978. Enumerative treatment of primary references includes Morrison's own book reviews, her nonfiction essays, and interviews as well as other articles containing her remarks.

368. Middleton, David L. *Toni Morrison: An Annotated Bibliography*. Garland Reference Library of the Humanities 767. New York: Garland, 1987.

Detailed coverage of writings by and about Morrison through 1985. Primary materials are presented by genre, then subarranged chronologically, with an enumerative list of the novels followed by separate sections for the periodical appearances of her nonfiction and interviews. Presentation of secondary citations divides itself between discussions of general topics and commentary on particular works. Scope of references is wide, extending to many ethnic, feminist, and local publications.

NABOKOV, VLADIMIR (1899-1977)

369. Zimmer, Dieter E. *Vladimir Nabokov: Bibliographie des Gesamtwerks*. Hamburg: Rowohlt Verlag, 1963. Rev. ed. 1964.

   Arranged chronologically by type, noting subsequent appearances of individual items and foreign editions. Coverage to early 1964.

370. Bryer, Jackson R., and Thomas J. Bergin, Jr. "Vladimir Nabokov's Critical Reputation in English: A Note and a Checklist." *Wisconsin Studies in Contemporary Literature* 8.2 (Spring 1967): 312-364.

   Offers thorough treatment of book reviews, review articles, and discussions of Nabokov in books. Most comprehensive for criticism appearing in periodicals.

371. Field, Andrew. "In Place of a Bibliography." In *Nabokov: His Life in Art*. Boston: Little, Brown, 1967, 352-380.

   Draws from, expands, and corrects Item 369. Later expanded into Item 372. Coverage to 1967.

372. ----------. *Nabokov: A Bibliography*. New York: McGraw-Hill, 1973.

   Comprehensive treatment of works by Nabokov into 1973. Unevenly annotated items are divided according to genre and include Nabokov's poetry (including translations of first lines of poems written in Russian), plays and scenarios, lepidoptera, chess problems, letters and interviews, and epigrams. Publication of individual pieces can be traced through subsequent appearances in anthologies, periodicals, and collections. Selected list of emigré reviews of Nabokov's works is arranged chronologically.

373. Parker, Stephen Jan, ed. "Bibliography." *The Vladimir Nabokov Research Newsletter* 1 (Fall 1978): 18-32. Continues in 2 (Spring 1979): 26-34; 3 (Fall 1979): 42-48; 4 (Spring 1980): 36-49; 5 (Fall 1980): 29-38; 6 (Spring 1981): 44-47; 7 (Fall 1981): 40-49; 11 (Fall 1983): 49-63. Resumes as the *Nabokovian* with 13 (Fall 1984): 45-59; continues in 15 (Fall 1985): 40-56; 17 (Fall 1986): 62-78; and 19 (Fall 1987): 61-79.

Organized to revise, complete, and update Item 372. It later performs the same function in relation to Item 376.

374. Schuman, Samuel. *Vladimir Nabokov: A Reference Guide*. Boston: G.K. Hall, 1979.

Organized chronologically, coverage extends to July 1977. Provides a comprehensive record of English-language critical articles and books on Nabokov. Offers a wide selection of works in foreign languages and samples of positive and negative book reviews and news stories. Lists doctoral dissertations, and includes masters theses if they were subsequently published or are widely recognized as important. Cross-references reprintings and revisions of critical items. Appendices incorporate a selection of criticism written in Russian and published in Russian-language periodicals, and a checklist of writings about movies based on Nabokov's works. Author, title, and character index.

375. Boyd, Brian. "Emigré Responses to Nabokov (I): 1921-1930." *Nabokovian* 17 (Fall 1986): 21-41; "Emigré Responses to Nabokov (II): 1931-1935." *Nabokovian* 18 (Spring 1987): 34-53.

Provides a chronological record of periodicals in which Nabokov's work appeared. Treatment expands, corrects, and increases number of entries found in Item 372.

376. Juliar, Michael. *Vladimir Nabokov: A Descriptive Bibliography.* Garland Reference Library of the Humanities 656. New York: Garland, 1986.

Near-exhaustive coverage through 1985 of all works by Nabokov. Arrangement is chronological by first appearance. Includes Russian, French, and English-language editions, as well as translations into other languages. Detailed physical descriptions and printing histories supplemented by photographs of dust jackets, title pages, and copyright pages. Other sections list braille and recorded editions, piracies, ephemerae, and prepublication items. Enumerative list of critical, biographical, and bibliographical sources arranged alphabetically by author; coverage deliberately excludes articles and book reviews. Appendices chronicle Nabokov's literary career and translations, the publication and reception of *Lolita*, and major Nabokov depositories.

NEARING, HOMER, JR. (1915-)

377. Purcell, Mark. "The Sinister Researches of C.P. Ransom: A Checklist." *Luna Monthly* 50 (Winter 1974): 3.

Enumerative record of original publication of stories in *Fantasy & Science Fiction* that were later collected in *The Sinister Researches of C. P. Ransom* (1954). Also lists five stories in the series which do not appear in *The Sinister Researches*. All stories were published during the period 1950-1956.

NEVINS, FRANCIS M. (1943-)

378. "Bibliography." In *St. Louis University Law Faculty Bibliography*. St. Louis: St. Louis University School of Law, 1987.

Enumerative checklist of Nevins's books, articles, and editorial work. Records publications through 1986. Previous editions of this bibliography have been issued.

NIN, ANAIS (1903-1977)

379. Hinz, Evelyn J. "Bibliography." In *The Mirror and the Garden: Realism and Reality in the Writings of Anais Nin*. Columbus: Publications Committee, Ohio State Univ. Libraries, 1971, 113-119.

   Valuable for unannotated but thorough checklist of secondary sources. Provides a wider range of book reviews than Item 385, although itself superseded by Item 386.

380. Zee, Nancy Scholar. "A Checklist of Nin Materials at Northwestern University Library." *Under the Sign of Pisces* 3.2 (Spring 1972): 3-11.

   Enumerates Nin's published and unpublished manuscripts.

381. Centing, Richard R. "Blurbs by Anais Nin." *Under the Sign of Pisces* 4.2 (Spring 1973). "Blurbs by Anais Nin: Part Two." *Under the Sign of Pisces* 12.3-4 (Summer-Fall 1981). "Blurbs by Anais Nin: Part Three." *Seahorse: The Anais Nin/Henry Miller Journal* 1.3 (16 September 1982): 13. "Blurbs by Anais Nin: Part Four." *Seahorse* 1.4 (25 December 1982): 6.

   Reprints each blurb in its entirety.

382. Franklin, Benjamin, V. "Anais Nin: A Bibliographical Essay." In *A Casebook of Anais Nin*. Ed. Robert Zaller. New York: NAL, 1974, 25-33.

   Focuses on problems in bibliographic research on Nin. Surveys books with variant titles, titles with variant contents, and titles that refer to more than one work.

383. ----------. *Anais Nin: A Bibliography*. Serif Series 29. Kent, Ohio: Kent State Univ. Press, 1974.

Arranged chronologically by type of material, treatment includes all English-language editions of Nin's works, with the exception of Canadian imprints. Separate sections list books and pamphlets, contributions to books and periodicals, editorship of periodicals, and nonprint materials. All items are fully annotated. An appendix notes letters written to Nin and published elsewhere. Thoroughly indexed.

384. Marcinczyk, Reesa. "A Checklist of the Writings of Anais Nin, 1973-1976." *Under the Sign of Pisces* 8.1 (Winter 1977): 2-14.

Designed to update and supplement Item 383, this list records Nin's books and their reviews, her contributions to books and journals, and her appearances in nonprint media.

385. "Selected Bibliography." In Benjamin Franklin V. and Duane Schneider, *Anais Nin: An Introduction*. Athens: Ohio Univ. Press, 1979, 301-304.

Contains useful evaluative list of articles and book-length studies of Nin. Sources chosen are those that present a balanced view of her art or are historically significant in her literary career. Essentially superseded by Item 386.

386. Cutting, Rose Marie. *Anais Nin: A Reference Guide*. Boston: G.K. Hall, 1978.

Records books and articles about Nin published between 1937 and 1977. Includes biographical items, interviews, and college newspaper and daily press articles. Does not note letters listed in Item 383. Often lengthy description of entries' scope and content. Arrangement is chronological. Title, author, and subject index.

387. Centing, Richard R. "Writings about Anais Nin: A First Supplement to Rose Marie Cutting's *Anais Nin: A Reference Guide*."

Under the Sign of Pisces 11.2 (Spring 1980): 1-12. Numbered series of supplements continues under same title in *Under the Sign of Pisces* 11.3 (Summer 1980): 9-24; 11.4 (Fall 1980): 14-23; 12.1 (Winter 1981): 1-15; 12.2 (Spring 1981): 1-22; 12.3-4 (Summer-Fall 1981): 18-24. Continues under same title in *Seahorse* 1.1 (21 February 1982): 12-16; 1.2 (4 July 1982): 5-9; 1.3 (16 September 1982): 1-5; 1.4 (25 December 1982): 1-6; 2.1 (1983): 10-12; 2.2 (1983): 7-12; 2.3 (1983): 8-11; 2.4 (1983): 18.

Arranged by type of secondary material, these checklists are designed to supplement Item 386. Annotations often reproduce lengthy portions of critical commentary or biographical accounts of Nin.

388. ----------. "Primary Nin: The First Checklist of Writings by Anais Nin." *Seahorse* 1.3 (16 September 1982): 14. A second "Checklist" appears in *Seahorse* 2.4 (1983): 17.

Enumerative record of primary writings by Nin not cited in previous bibliographies.

NIVEN, LARRY (1938-)

389. Drumm, Chris. *Larry Niven Checklist*. Polk City, Iowa: Chris Drumm, 1983.

Chronological listing of writings published through 1983, noting forthcoming titles and works in progress. Provides information on prices, reprintings, collaborations, and series. Often lists foreign-language editions.

NOLAN, WILLIAM F. (1928-)

*390. Nolan, William F. "Nolan Mystery Checklist." *Armchair Detective* 3 (1969/70): 26-27.

Albert in Item 2 notes that this checklist, compiled by the author, registers Nolan's fiction and non-fiction mystery writing.

*391. Yenter, Charles E. *William F. Nolan: A Checklist*. Tacoma, Wash.: Charles E. Yenter, 1974.

Cited in Item 40.

*392. Clarke, Boden, and James Hopkins. *The Work of William F. Nolan: An Annotated Bibliography & Guide*. Bibliographies of Modern Authors 14. San Bernardino, Calif.: Borgo Press, forthcoming, 1988.

Recorded in Item 40; currently being catalogued at the Library of Congress.

NORTON, ANDRE (1912-)

*393. Lofland, Robert D. "Andre Norton: A Contemporary Author of Books for Young People." M.A. Thesis. Kent State Univ. 1960.

Roger C. Schlobin in Item 401 states that Lofland provides a checklist of Norton's writings through 1959.

*394. ----------. "Andre Norton: A Bibliography 1934-1963." M.L.S. Thesis. Univ. of California at Los Angeles, 1963.

Records annotated coverage of primary works to 1963. Cited in Item 401.

*395. Wilbur, Sharon. "Andre Norton: Her Life and Writings with an Analysis of Her Science Fiction and an Annotated Bibliography." M.L.S. Thesis. Texas Women's University, 1966.

Listed in Item 401.

*396. Peters, Becky D. "A Bio-Bibliographical Study of Andre Norton, 1960-1971." M.A. Thesis. Kent State University, 1971.

Schlobin in Item 401 reports that this is a continuation of Item 393.

397. Norton, Andre. "Norton Bibliography." In *The Many Worlds of Andre Norton*. Ed. Roger Elwood. Radnor, Pa.: Chilton, 1974, 201-208.

Provides an enumerative checklist of writings by Norton. Materials are arranged alphabetically within genres, including short stories, collections of stories, collaborations, and book-length publications. Publishing information records series to which each item belongs, first American editions, and selected subsequent foreign-language reprintings. Also notes pseudonyms and title changes.

*398. [Turner, David G.] *The First Editions of Andre Norton*. Menlo Park, Calif.: David G. Turner, Bookman, 1974.

Chronological coverage of primary writings to 1973. Cited in Item 401.

399. Hewitt, Helen-Jo Jakusz. "Andre Norton Bibliography." In *The Book of Andre Norton*. Ed. Roger Elwood. New York: DAW Books, 1975, 211-221.

A revision of Item 397, this checklist lists individual items' subject matter or theme. Includes a list of anthologies edited by Norton. Coverage, like that of Item 397, is to 1974.

400. Miesel, Sandra. "Bibliography of Andre Norton's Witch World." In *Witch World*. Boston: Gregg Press, 1977.

An alphabetical listing by title of books and stories forming part of Norton's Witch World series. Unannotated.

401. Schlobin, Roger C. *Andre Norton: A Primary and Secondary Bibliography*. Boston: G.K. Hall, 1980.

Records works by and about Norton through June 1979. Chronologically arranged sections list fiction (first editions, collections, edited anthologies, short stories), poetry, and nonfiction. Notes textual variants, abridgements, pseudonyms, and subsequent publications of individual items. Coverage of secondary sources includes biographical and critical pieces, and substantive reviews; entries are fully annotated. Indexes primary works by title, secondary studies by author. Appendices arrange primary works by genre and record interrelationships between Norton's works of fiction.

OATES, JOYCE CAROL (1938-)

402. McCormick, Lucienne. "A Bibliography of Works by and about Joyce Carol Oates." *American Literature* 43.1 (March 1971): 124-132.

Arranged by type of material, noting subsequent editions of books by Oates. Treatment does not allow tracing of publication of individual items. Selective list of secondary sources, primarily book reviews, organized alphabetically by book title. Excludes Oates' own book reviews. Coverage into 1970.

403. Catron, Douglas. "A Contribution to a Bibliography of Works by and about Joyce Carol Oates." *American Literature* 49.3 (November 1977): 399-414.

Reproduces format of Item 402, extending coverage to 1976. Significantly expands number of articles about Oates noted in Item 402. Superseded by Item 405 in depth and detail of coverage.

404. Dickinson, Donald. "Joyce Carol Oates: A Bibliographical Checklist." *American Book Collector* ns 2.6 (November-December 1981): 26-39. Continued in *American Book Collector* ns 3.1 (January-February 1982): 42-48.

Coverage extends into 1981. Describes the history and physical appearance of Oates's primary writings. Notes first, English, and limited or signed editions. Treatment includes broadsides and printed cards. Continuation of coverage focuses on Oates' individual stories, verse, and miscellaneous writings (response to a questionnaire, interviews, introductions, and one published statement). Entries are annotated. Misses some of Oates' essays appearing in books other than her own.

405. Lercangée, Francine, and Bruce F. Michelson. *Joyce Carol Oates: An Annotated Bibliography.* Garland Reference Library of the Humanities 509. New York: Garland, 1986.

Comprehensive, partially annotated treatment of writings by and about Oates through August 1985. Primary materials, arranged alphabetically by type, include novels, stories, poems, plays, anthologies edited, nonfiction, and interviews. Entries for essays and other nonfiction summarize critical arguments. Notes original appearances of individual items, reprintings, and English editions. Book-length studies of Oates are listed chronologically and described in detail; a checklist of critical articles in books and periodicals, organized according to the Oates book discussed, also includes foreign-language items. Includes doctoral dissertations. Author, title, periodical, and subject index.

O'CONNOR, FLANNERY (1925-1964)

406. Wedge, George F. "Two Bibliographies: Flannery O'Connor/J.F. Powers." *Critique* 2.2 (Fall 1958): 59-70, esp. 59-63.

Enumerative record of primary works, arranged alphabetically. Treatment notes subsequent printings of individual items. Also lists reviews and critical studies of O'Connor's writings.

407. Lawson, Lewis A. "Bibliography." In *The Added Dimension: The Art and Mind of Flannery O'Connor.* Ed. Melvin J. Friedman and Lewis A. Lawson. New York: Fordham Univ. Press, 1966, 281-302. 2nd ed. 1977.

Provides separate alphabetical and chronological listings of individual works. Includes translations and a chronological record of book editions. Secondary sources are divided into book reviews (arranged by title), criticism, and interviews; entries found here complement those provided in Item 409. Coverage to fall 1965; 2nd edition reprints 1966 checklist without revision.

408. Brittain, Joan T. "Flannery O'Connor: A Bibliography." *Bulletin of Bibliography* 25.4 (September-December 1967): 98-100. Continued in *Bulletin of Bibliography* 25.5 (January-April 1968): 123-124. See also "Flannery O'Connor: Addenda." *Bulletin of Bibliography* 25.6 (May-August 1968): 142.

Provides a chronological checklist of O'Connor's fiction, noting subsequent appearances of stories and reprintings of books. Contents of collections are enumerated. O'Connor's nonfiction is arranged alphabetically by title; biographical and critical writings on O'Connor are listed alphabetically by author. Part 2 completes coverage of secondary sources through late 1965. Entries are unannotated.

409. "Bibliography." In Leon V. Driskell and Joan T. Brittain, *The Eternal Crossroads: The Art of Flannery O'Connor*. Lexington: Univ. Press of Kentucky, 1971, 151-165.

Unannotated checklist of works by and about O'Connor. Critical articles and reviews listed alphabetically by author; separate section records biographical treatments.

410. Becham, Gerald. "Flannery O'Connor Collection." *Flannery O'Connor Bulletin* 1 (Autumn 1972): 66-71.

Chronological survey of materials held by Georgia College.

411. Lackey, Allen. "Flannery O'Connor: A Supplemental Bibliography of Secondary Sources." *Bulletin of Bibliography* 30.4 (October-December 1973): 170-175.

Designed to supplement and make corrections to Items 407, 408, and 409. Thorough coverage through 1972.

412. Dorsey, James E. "Carson McCullers and Flannery O'Connor: A Checklist of Graduate Research." *Bulletin of Bibliography* 32.4 (October-December 1975): 162-167.

Compilation of graduate dissertations based primarily on standard indexes and intended to supplement previously published bibliographies. Most useful for its listing of masters theses. Research on O'Connor is chronicled into early 1975. Separate section lists works dealing with both authors.

413. Golden, Robert E. "Flannery O'Connor: A Reference Guide." In *Flannery O'Connor and Caroline Gordon: A Reference Guide.* Ed. Robert E. Golden and Mary C. Sullivan. Boston: G.K. Hall, 1977, 1-186.

Comprehensive coverage of secondary materials, excluding transient mentions and items in standard reference works, for the period 1952-1976. Some foreign-language items and reprintings of major articles and reviews are included. Especially valuable for its record of doctoral dissertations through 1975. Annotations describe scope and argument of items.

414. Getz, Lorine M. *Flannery O'Connor: Her Life, Library and Book Reviews.* New York: Edwin Mellen Press, 1980.

First section reprints O'Connor's published and unpublished book reviews; cross-referenced with list of books reviewed by O'Connor.

415. Farmer, David R. *Flannery O'Connor: A Descriptive Bibliography.* Garland Reference Library of the Humanities 221. New York: Garland, 1981.

Supplements coverage of all published writings by O'Connor with a number of her illustrations, primarily linoleum block-cut cartoons. Books are listed in order of publication and include later editions or impressions. Special attention has been paid to dates of republication and press run figures. Notes stories, college writings and contributions to books written by others; an additional section records adaptations, films, and parodies based on O'Connor's works. Deliberately excludes reprints in college texts and anthologies and a list of manuscript holdings. Indicates that the coverage of translations may be incomplete.

416. Getz, Lorine M. "Bibliography." In *Nature and Grace in Flannery O'Connor's Fiction*. Studies in Art and Religious Interpretation 2. New York: Edwin Mellen Press, 1982, 155-174.

Enumerative checklist of works by and about O'Connor. Notes unpublished lectures and presentations, supplementing Item 413. Also useful for its emphasis in secondary section on religious aspects of O'Connor's life and work.

OLIVER, CHAD (1928-)

417. Nolan, William F. "Chad Oliver's Collected Science Fiction: A Basic Checklist." In Chad Oliver, *The Edge of Forever: Classic Anthropological Science Fiction*. Los Angeles: Sherbourne Press, 1971, 301-305.

Lists stories, novels, and collaborations in chronological order, noting contents of Oliver's one collection. Anthology appearances recorded alphabetically by editor. Cites two stories collected outside the U.S. Provides coverage for the years 1950-1971.

*418. Hall, H. W. *The Work of Chad Oliver: An Annotated Bibliography and Guide*. Bryan, Tx.: Dellwood Press, 1985.

In the process of being catalogued by the Library of Congress. Cited in volume 2 of H. W. Hall's *Science Fiction and Fantasy Reference Index, 1878-1985: An International Author and Subject Index to History and Criticism* (Detroit: Gale Research, 1987).

ORTIZ, SIMON (1941-)

419. Ruoff, Lavonne Brown. "Simon Ortiz: S.A.I.L. Bibliography #7." *Studies in American Indian Literature* 8.3-4 (Summer-Fall 1984): 57-58.

> Records Ortiz's poetry, fiction, and nonfiction. Enumerative treatment.

OZICK, CYNTHIA (1928-)

420. Currier, Susan, and Daniel J. Cahill. "A Bibliography of Writings by Cynthia Ozick." *Texas Studies in Literature and Language* 25.2 (Summer 1983): 313-321. Revised under same title in *Contemporary American Women Writers: Narrative Strategies*. Ed. Catherine Rainwater and William J. Scheick. Lexington: Univ. Press of Kentucky, 1985, 109-116.

> Enumerative checklist of works by Ozick, including stories, poems, articles, and reviews, arranged chronologically. Reprintings of individual items are recorded. Treats works published through early 1983. Revised version extends coverage into summer 1983 with a few entries from 1984.

421. Chenoweth, Mary J. "Bibliographical Essay: Cynthia Ozick." *Studies in American Jewish Literature* 6 (Fall 1987): 147-163.

> Provides a narrative survey of Ozick's background, published novels, uncollected stories, collections of stories, and works appearing in anthologies. Also records Ozick's poems, translations, and essays. Briefly surveys critical responses to Ozick and lists reviews grouped by individual title.

PALEY, GRACE (1922-)

422. Hulley, Kathleen. "Bibliography on Grace Paley." *Delta* 14 (May 1982): 147-150.

Enumerative listing of primary works. Short stories deemed more accessible in anthologies have not been recorded as individual items. Valuable for treatment of secondary materials.

423. Schleifer, Ronald. "A Bibliography of Writings by Grace Paley." In *Contemporary American Women Writers: Narrative Strategies*. Ed. Catherine Rainwater and William J. Scheick. Lexington: Univ. Press of Kentucky, 1985, 48-49.

> Treats Paley's writings through 1985. Separate sections record books, uncollected short stories, articles, and miscellaneous items (primarily interviews).

PANGBORN, EDGAR (1909-1976)

*424. Benson, Gordon, Jr. *Edgar Pangborn: A Bibliography*. Albuquerque: Galactic Central, 1985.

> Volume 2 of H. W. Hall's *Science Fiction and Fantasy Reference Index, 1878-1985: An International Author and Subject Index to History and Criticism* (Detroit: Gale Research, 1987) registers this study.

PARKER, ROBERT B. (1932-)

*425. Hoffman, Carl. "Spenser: The Illusion of Knighthood." *Armchair Detective* 16 (1983): 131-138, 140-143.

> According to Albert in Item 2, this article contains a bibliography of primary and secondary materials.

PERCY, WALKER (1916-)

426. Byrd, Scott, and John F. Zeugner. "Walker Percy: A Checklist." *Bulletin of Bibliography* 30.1 (January-March 1973): 16-17, 44.

> Chronological checklist of Percy's college articles, essays, book reviews, interviews, and American editions of his novels. Foreign editions and blurbs have been deliberately excluded.

Entries are unannotated and subsequent appearances of individual items, if any, are not recorded.

427. Weixlmann, Joe, and Daniel H. Gann. "A Walker Percy Bibliography." *Southern Quarterly* 18.3 (1980): 137-157. Reprinted in *Walker Percy: Art and Ethics*. Jackson: Univ. Press of Mississippi, 1980, 137-157.

Chronological listing of Percy's publications and reviews of them. Thorough coverage also records Percy's shorter works, interviews, and printed remarks. Secondary sources are arranged alphabetically by author and divided according to type of material (including dissertations and theses).

428. "Walker Percy: A Selected Bibliography." *Delta* 13 (November 1981): 177-187.

Reproduces arrangement of Item 427, with coverage to early 1981. Reviews, newspaper accounts, and brief mentions of Percy have been excluded.

429. Kramer, Victor A., et al. *Andrew Lytle, Walker Percy, Peter Taylor: A Reference Guide*. Boston: G.K. Hall, 1983, esp. 61-186.

Records writings about Percy, including dissertations and theses, for the period 1961-1980. Arrangement is chronological, then alphabetical by author. Annotations summarize scope and argument of critical items.

430. Wright, Stuart. *Walker Percy: A Bibliography, 1930-1984*. Westport, Ct.: Meckler, 1986.

This descriptive bibliography treats Percy's separate publications, publications in books and nonserial items, periodical appearances, and interviews and published commentary. Comprehensive and detailed coverage includes physical description and publishing history of individual items. Chronological arrangement.

PERELMAN, S. J. (1904-1979)

431. Gale, Steven H. "Sidney Joseph Perelman: Twenty Years of American Humor." *Bulletin of Bibliography* 29.1 (January-March 1972): 10-12.

Unannotated coverage of Perelman's publications in major American periodicals and books published between 1940 and 1960. Arrangement is alphabetical by title. Incorporated in Item 432.

432. ----------. *S. J. Perelman: An Annotated Bibliography.* Garland Reference Library of the Humanities 531. New York: Garland, 1985.

Enumerative checklist of works by and about Perelman. Arrangement is chronological and divided according to type of material. Coverage includes television scripts, recordings, incidental pieces, and letters. Entries note contents of collections and allow tracing of publication of individual items. Materials that could not be dated and items not located using information in other sources have been indicated. Selective annotated checklist of scholarly criticism, including papers delivered at professional meetings, extends through mid-1984. Appendix' lists Perelman materials held by the University of Pittsburgh. Separate indexes provide chronological lists of Perelman's writings and critical responses to his works.

PETRY, ANN (1911-)

433. Hill, James Lee. "Bibliography of the Works of Chester Himes, Ann Petry and Frank Yerby." *Black Books Bulletin* 3.3 (1975): 60-72, esp. 65-68.

Enumerative checklist arranges Petry's stories, novels, and non-fiction by title. Secondary sources include biographical and critical studies; arguments of the critical pieces are summarized.

PIERCY, MARGE (1936-)

434. Hansen, Elaine Tuttle, and William J. Scheick. "A Bibliography of Writings by Marge Piercy." In *Contemporary American Women Writers: Narrative Strategies*. Ed. Catherine Rainwater and William J. Scheick. Lexington: Univ. Press of Kentucky, 1985, 224-228.

Enumerative record of Piercy's books, stories, articles, and miscellaneous materials, among them a number of recordings, published through 1983. Individual citations of poems have been omitted.

PIPER, H. BEAM (1904-1964)

435. Espley, John L. "H. Beam Piper: An Annotated Bibliography." *Extrapolation* 21.2 (Summer 1980): 172-181.

Records comprehensive coverage of works by Piper. Sections treat Piper's books, magazine appearances, publications in anthologies, and reviews of his writings. Reprintings, including many foreign-language editions, are listed. Annotations provide plot summaries of stories and novels and assess the quality of each piece.

PLANTE, DAVID (1940-)

436. Bixby, George. "David Plante: A Bibliographical Checklist." *American Book Collector* ns 5.6 (November-December 1984): 25-28.

Provides descriptive record of both major and minor appearances by Plante. Notes first American and British editions, individual stories, and miscellaneous writings published through 1984.

PORTER, BERN (1911-)

437. Simon, Renee B. "Bern Porter: A Bibliographical Sampling." *Colby Library Quarterly* 9.2 (June 1970): 105-113.

> Chronological record of works published by Porter, noting degree of his involvement in each production. Does not include Porter's own writing.

POTOK, CHAIM (1929-)

438. Fagerheim, Cynthia. "Chaim Potok: A Bibliographic Essay." *Studies in American Jewish Literature* 4 (1985): 107-120.

> Summarizes publication and critical reception of Potok's writings. Biographical and bibliographical items cited are generally limited to references from standard sources.

439. Abramson, Edward A. "Selected Bibliography." In *Chaim Potok*. Twayne's United States Authors Series 503. Boston: G.K. Hall, 1986, 150-155.

> Enumerative record arranges Potok's novels and short stories alphabetically, his essays and book reviews chronologically. Useful selection of secondary sources accompanied by contents notes. Coverage to 1985.

POWERS, J. F. (1917-)

440. Wedge, George F. "Two Bibliographies: Flannery O'Connor/J.F. Powers." *Critique* 2.2 (Fall 1958): 59-70, esp. 63-70.

> Writings by Powers are arranged alphabetically by type, except for magazine pieces which are listed chronologically. A thorough, unannotated checklist that also records reviews and critical assessments of Powers's writings.

441. Padilla, Carlos Villalobos. "Bibliography." In *The Art of Short Fiction in J.F. Powers*. Ph.D. Diss. Universidad Nacional Autonoma de Mexico, 1963, 113-119.

Registers the first American and English editions of Powers's short story collections, listing contents of each. A separate section treats stories published in magazines and anthologies. Extends Item 440's coverage of short fiction to 1963. Secondary sources are unannotated.

442. Meyers, Jeffrey. "J.F. Powers: Uncollected Stories, Essays and Interviews, 1943-1979." *Bulletin of Bibliography* 44.1 (March 1987): 38-39.

Enumerative chronological record of individual items, noting reprintings.

PRICE, REYNOLDS (1933-)

*443. Owens, Clayton S. "Reynolds Price: A Bibliography." M.A. Thesis. Univ. of North Carolina, Chapel Hill, 1976.

Item 445 reports that Owens' work was a source for their own bibliography.

444. Roberts, Ray. "Reynolds Price: A Bibliographical Checklist." *American Book Collector* ns 2.4 (July-August 1981): 15-23.

Chronological treatment of separate publications by Price, including poems, statements, an interview and drawing, and introductions for other writers' works. Records physical descriptions and limited publication information. Does not treat Price's periodical contributions. Coverage into 1981.

445. Wright, Stuart, and James L.W. West III. *Reynolds Price: A Bibliography 1949-1984*. Pub. for the Bibliographical Society of the University of Virginia. Charlottesville: Univ. Press of Virginia, 1986.

Comprehensive coverage of works published by Price up through 1984. Fully descriptive treatment of first impressions of first American editions. Notes subsequent appearance of individual items. Separate sections list contributions to books, periodical and newspaper appearances, and translations. Interviews, published discussions and comments, and miscellaneous items are recorded. Arrangement is chronological by type of material. Author and title index. Based in part on Items 443, and 444.

PRONZINI, BILL (1943-)

446. Nevins, Francis, Jr., and Bill Pronzini. "Bill Pronzini: A Checklist." *Armchair Detective* 13 (1980): 345-350.

Provides a chronological record of books and anthologies written or co-authored by Pronzini through 1979. Other sections treat his short fiction, including pieces published in collaboration with Michael Kurland, Barry N. Malzberg, and Jeffrey Wallmann. Accompanied by reproductions of book jackets.

*447. "Bibliographie" for "Dossier Bill Pronzini." *Polar* 20 (July 1981): 17-19.

This checklist is recorded in Item 2, but could not be located.

PURDY, JAMES (1923-)

448. Bush, George E. "James Purdy." *Bulletin of Bibliography* 28.1 (January-March 1971): 5-6.

Covers the period 1956-1971. Alphabetical listing of individual works followed by citations of secondary materials about them. Separate section treats general criticism on Purdy. Entries not annotated. Remains valuable for coverage of secondary sources.

449. Ladd, Jay. "James Purdy: A Bibliography Checklist." *American Book Collector* ns 2.5 (September-October 1981): 53-60.

Comprehensive treatment of separate publications by Purdy published through 1981. Notes first American and English editions, physical descriptions, and contents of collections, but does not record Purdy's contributions to periodicals.

PYNCHON, THOMAS (1937-)

450. Weixlmann, Joseph. "Thomas Pynchon: A Bibliography." *Critique* 14.2 (1972): 34-43.

Chronological checklist of works by and about Pynchon. Book reviews follow entries for novels, and only reviews containing interpretations of substantiated value judgments are indicated. Secondary materials arranged in the following categories: biography, criticism of individual works, general studies, and bibliographies published in standard reference sources. Coverage to 1972.

451. Herzberg, Bruce. "Selected Articles on Thomas Pynchon: An Annotated Bibliography." *Twentieth-Century Literature* 21.2 (May 1975): 221-225.

Provides analytical entries for critical articles; selected book reviews are not annotated. Covers the period 1963-1975.

452. ----------. "Bibliography [of Pynchon]." In *Mindful Pleasures: Essays on Thomas Pynchon*. Ed. George Levine and David Leverenz. Boston: Little, Brown, 1976, 265-269.

Enumerative checklist intended to supplement Item 450. Unannotated list of primary works is accompanied by a selective record of book reviews and critical articles published between 1972 and fall 1975. A separate section treats general studies that include criticism on Pynchon.

453. Scotto, Robert M. *Three Contemporary Novelists: An Annotated Bibliography of Works by and about John Hawkes, Joseph Heller,*

and Thomas Pynchon. Garland Reference Library of the Humanities 52. New York: Garland, 1977.

Provides a chronological listing of Pynchon's novels limited to American editions, noting important revisions and reprintings. Other primary materials are recorded alphabetically by title and include uncollected items and interviews. Selectively annotated coverage of secondary sources treats reviews, critical and biographical studies, special issues of journals, bibliographies, and dissertations.

454. Walsh, Thomas P., and Cameron Northouse. *John Barth, Jerzy Kosinski, and Thomas Pynchon: A Reference Guide*. Boston: G.K. Hall, 1977, esp. 93-132.

Most valuable for chronological record of secondary materials about Pynchon for the period 1963-1975. Annotations are descriptive. Pynchon sources are indexed separately.

455. *Pynchon Notes* 1.1- (October 1979-).

Features of this ongoing newsletter include critical works-in-progress, circulating manuscripts, and forthcoming essays, book-length studies, dissertations, and symposium papers on Pynchon. Records works by and about Pynchon that have not been included in previous bibliographical studies listed above as Items 450, 451, 452, 453, and 454.

456. Monahan, Matthew. "Thomas Pynchon: A Bibliographical Checklist." *American Book Collector* ns 5.3 (May-June 1984): 37-39.

Physical descriptions and printing information accompany this enumerative list of separately published writings by Pynchon. Section A notes first U.S. and English editions of novels; section B lists stories and an introduction written by Pynchon. Coverage extends into 1984.

QUENTIN, PATRICK (1912-)

*457. "Patrick Quentin." *Les Amis du crime* 2 (n.d.): n.p.

> Albert in Item 2 states that this issue contains a bibliography of the fiction published by Hugh Wheeler, best known as Patrick Quentin, who also published under the pseudonyms Q. Patrick and Jonathan Stagge. Treatment includes a filmography and a grouping of Wheeler's books by pseudonym.

REDMON, ANNE (1943-)

458. Rainwater, Catherine. "A Bibliography of Writings by Anne Redmon." In *Contemporary American Women Writers: Narrative Strategies*. Ed. Catherine Rainwater and William J. Scheick. Lexington: Univ. Press of Kentucky, 1985, 84-86.

> Enumerative coverage to 1981 of Redmon's fiction and many book reviews. Annotations supply names of authors and books discussed when not included in the titles of her reviews. Arrangement is chronological.

REED, ISHMAEL (1938-)

459. Settle, Elizabeth A., and Robert A. Settle. *Ishmael Reed: An Annotated Checklist*. E.R.C. Occasional Papers 1. Carson: California State College, Dominquez Hills, 1977.

> A preliminary bibliography that attempts comprehensive coverage of works by Reed. Records Reed's nonprint materials, original appearances of individual items, and poems printed separately in anthologies or in Reed's collections. Purports to list all critical commentary and biographical entries published on Reed through 1977. Thoroughly indexed. Essentially superseded by Item 461.

460. Weixlmann, Joe, Robert Fikes, Jr., and Ishmael Reed. "Mapping Out the Gumbo Works: An Ishmael Reed Bibliography." *Black American Literature Forum* 12.1 (Spring 1978): 24-29.

Comprehensive treatment of works by and about Reed through mid-1977. Chronological entries for novels, anthologies, and books of poetry note editions and reviews. Lists uncollected poems and stories, and Reed's essays and book reviews. Also records printed remarks and miscellaneous items. Separate section records general critical studies; remaining secondary materials grouped by the title they treat. Deliberately excludes ephemeral biographical mentions of Reed.

461. Settle, Elizabeth A., and Robert A. Settle. *Ishmael Reed: A Primary and Secondary Bibliography*. Boston: G.K. Hall, 1982.

Chronological coverage of works by and about Reed through 1980, with a few items from 1981. Includes nonprint media as well as original and anthology appearances of Reed's poems. Annotations summarize argument and tenor of critical studies. Thorough index.

REYNOLDS, MACK (1917-1983)

462. Drumm, Chris, and George Flynn. *A Mack Reynolds Checklist*. Polk City, Iowa: Chris Drumm, 1983.

Provides chronological record of stories and novels. Notes collaborations, title changes, and reprintings. Coverage to early 1983.

ROTH, PHILIP (1933-)

463. McDaniel, John N. "Philip Roth: A Checklist 1954-73." *Bulletin of Bibliography* 31.2 (April-June 1974): 51-53.

Unannotated checklist of works by and about Roth through March 1973. Notes paperback reprintings and portions of novels published separately. Records Roth's articles, symposia, and interviews; primary writings are divided according to genre. Thorough coverage of secondary sources arranged alphabetically by author.

464. Rodgers, Bernard F., Jr. *Philip Roth: A Bibliography.* 2nd ed. Scarecrow Author Bibliographies 19. Metuchen, N.J.: Scarecrow Press, 1984. 1st ed. 1974.

Comprehensive coverage of primary materials extends to 1983. Enumerative checklist notes foreign-language translations, juvenilia, play and screenplay adaptations of Roth's works, original periodical appearances of stories, and letters to the editor. Based in part on holdings in Roth's personal library. Annotated secondary section arranged topically, including foreign reviews (written in English) and unpublished doctoral dissertations. Treatment doubles the primary items and quadruples the secondary items in Item 463.

RUMAKER, MICHAEL (1932-)

465. Butterick, George. "Michael Rumaker: A Checklist." *Athanor* 6 (Spring 1975): 45-49.

Very thorough coverage of works by Rumaker into 1974. Books, contributions to anthologies, and periodical appearances are arranged chronologically in separate sections. Treatment is notable for its record of translations and reprintings of individual items.

SALINGER, J. D. (1919-)

466. Davis, Tom. "J. D. Salinger: A Checklist." *Papers of the Bibliographical Society of America* 53.1 (January-March 1959): 69-71.

Records works published by Salinger from 1940 through 1957. This enumerative checklist also lists critical reviews and essays written about Salinger during the period July 1951-February 1959.

*467. Fiene, Donald M. "A Bibliographical Study of J.D. Salinger: Life, Work, and Reputation." M.A. Thesis. Univ. of Louisville, 1961.

Item 471 reports that Fiene's annotated study comprehensively surveys works by and about Salinger. According to Sublette, this is the first Salinger bibliography to contain foreign-language editions of primary writings and critical studies. Condensed as Item 468.

468. ----------. "J.D. Salinger: A Bibliography." *Wisconsin Studies in Contemporary Literature* 4 (Winter 1963): 109-149.

An abridged version of Item 467. Thorough treatment of works by and about Salinger. Notes translations, original appearances, and reprintings of primary items. Secondary sources include some foreign-language book reviews.

469. Starosciak, Kenneth. *J. D. Salinger: A Thirty Year Bibliography 1938-1968*. St. Paul, Minn.: Croixide Press, 1971.

Arranges primary and secondary entries chronologically; provides alphabetical index of authors. Extremely thorough treatment of secondary sources: critical collections, individual articles, and book reviews (organized by book). Omits most doctoral dissertations, some book reviews, and brief references to Salinger.

470. Bixby, George. "J. D. Salinger: A Bibliographical Checklist." *American Book Collector* ns 2.3 (May-June 1981): 29-32.

Thorough coverage into 1963 of writings by Salinger. Detailed entries for Salinger's books, stories, and autobiographical statement supplemented by record of pirated editions of story collections.

471. Sublette, Jack. *J. D. Salinger: An Annotated Bibliography*. Garland Reference Library of the Humanities 436. New York: Garland, 1984.

Comprehensive enumerative record of works by and about Salinger for the period 1938-1981. Contents notes summarize argument, scope, and tone of secondary materials. Author and title index.

SAPIR, RICHARD (1936-)

472. Murray, Will. "The Destroyer Series." *Paperback Quarterly* (Winter 1981).

Supplements a narrative account of the creation and publication of this series, with a chronological checklist of individual titles. Treatment identifies those books written individually or in collaboration by Sapir, Richard S. Meyers, Robert Randisi, William Ted Joy, and Molly Cochran.

SAROYAN, WILLIAM (1908-1981)

473. Kherdian, David. *A Bibliography of William Saroyan 1934-1964*. San Francisco: Roger Beacham, 1965.

Treatment of books includes first and special editions, subsequent printings, and most important British editions, noting title changes and textual variants. Separate sections list fugitive pieces and ephemerae, paperback reprints, sheet music, piano-vocal scores, and recordings. Enumerates original appearances of essays, articles, stories, fables, and notes in book form; with a few exceptions, excludes contributions to periodicals and newspapers. Saroyan's plays are arranged chronologically by first appearance in print. Highly selective treatment of secondary sources consists of articles in periodicals and important references in books. Well indexed.

SARTON, MAY (1912-)

474. Blouin, Lenora P. *May Sarton: A Bibliography*. Scarecrow Author Bibliographies 34. Metuchen, N.J.: Scarecrow Press, 1978.

Thorough coverage of works by and about Sarton through 1976. Arranges materials chronologically by type, with the exception of uncollected poems, which are listed alphabetically by title.

Registers anthology appearances and translations by Sarton, as well as film scripts, recordings, letters, and manuscripts. Offers plot summaries of novels. Selective listing of secondary sources divided into book reviews, biographical studies, and critical treatments. Foreign-language criticism has been deliberately omitted. Entries give critical arguments and overall tone of reviews and articles. Appendix provides alphabetical checklist of all poems cross-referenced with main entries. Notes that some individual poems and book reviews may have been missed.

475. ----------. "Bibliography." In *May Sarton: Woman and Poet*. Ed. Constance Hunting. The Man and Poet Series 4. Orono: National Poetry Foundation, Univ. of Maine at Orono, 1982, 283-319.

Reproduces format and extends coverage of Item 474 into 1982.

SAVAGE, ERNEST (1918-)

*476. Lachman, Marvin. "Department of Unknown Mystery Writers." *Poisoned Pen* 4.3 (June 1981): 11-13. See also Robert Randisi and Edward D. Hoch's addenda in *Poisoned Pen* 4.5-6 (December 1981): 83, 99.

Item 2 reports that this article includes a checklist of Savage's stories published in *Ellery Queen's Mystery Magazine* and *Alfred Hitchcock's Mystery Magazine*.

SCHMITZ, JAMES H. (1911-1981)

477. Owings, Mark. *James H. Schmitz: A Bibliography*. Baltimore: Croatan House, 1973.

Enumerative checklist of Schmitz's fiction is arranged alphabetically. Records contents of short story collections, original publications of stories, and subsequent reprintings of individual items.

SHOCKLEY, ANN ALLEN (1927-)

478. Dandridge, Rita B. *Ann Allen Shockley: An Annotated Primary and Secondary Bibliography*. Bibliographies and Indexes in Afro-American and African Studies 18. Westport, Ct.: Greenwood Press, 1987.

Lists comprehensively all published and unpublished works by Shockley through 1985. Treats Shockley's fiction and nonfiction, often providing lengthy summaries and thematic analyses of individual items. Coverage of secondary sources includes biographical accounts, critical assessments, and citations for the most easily accessible reviews of Shockley's life and works.

SILVERBERG, ROBERT (1936-)

479. Tuck, Donald H. "A Silverberg Bibliography." *Magazine of Fantasy and Science Fiction* 46.4 (April 1974): 81-88.

Provides an enumerative checklist of Silverberg's fiction and nonfiction. Arrangement is alphabetical within genre. Publication information includes original printings of individual items, Silverberg's collaborations, and his pseudonyms.

480. Justice, Keith L. "Background and Checklist: Don Elliott/Robert Silverberg Erotic Fiction Titles." *Megavore* 13 (March 1981): 18-24.

Comprehensive listing of softcore pornography and erotic fiction published by Silverberg during the period 1959-1965. Arrangement is by imprint group. Notes the number of pages and cover price of each item and provides some physical descriptions. Treatment, designed to supplement the coverage of Item 481, is accompanied by many reproductions of book covers.

481. Clareson, Thomas D. *Robert Silverberg: A Primary and Secondary Bibliography*. Boston: G.K. Hall, 1983.

Comprehensive coverage of works by and about Silverberg into 1981. Arranges primary materials chronologically by genre, noting pseudonyms and original pagination. Also lists works edited, nonfiction, miscellaneous fiction, and his writings on science fiction. Annotated secondary section treats book reviews and major English-language studies of Silverberg's works. Appendices record: Silverberg's articles in *Bulletin of the Science Fiction Writers of America*; pseudonymous works; and awards and nominations.

SIMAK, CLIFFORD D. (1904-1988)

*482. Owings, Mark. "Electric Bibliograph." *WSFA Journal* 66 (April-May 1969).

Becker in Item 484 reports that this checklist records first editions, reprints, title changes, and some translations of Simak's works.

*483. ----------. *The Electric Bibliograph, Part I: Clifford D. Simak*. Baltimore: Produced by Alice and Jay Haldeman, 1971.

Robert E. Briney and Edward Wood state in *SF Bibliographies: An Annotated Bibliography of Bibliographical Works on Science Fiction and Fantasy Fiction* (Chicago: Advent, 1972) that this monograph is an expanded version of Item 482.

484. Becker, Muriel R. *Clifford D. Simak: A Primary and Secondary Bibliography*. Boston: G.K. Hall, 1980.

A comprehensive account of Simak's writings published from December 1931 through November 1978, arranged chronologically by type of material. Coverage of secondary materials is for the period 1939-1978. Valuable for its annotated appendices which treat Simak's book club titles, title changes, anthology appearances, and manuscripts. Well indexed.

SINGER, ISAAC BASHEVIS (1904-)

485. Buchen, Irving H. "Bibliography." In *Isaac Bashevis Singer and the Eternal Past*. New York: New York Univ. Press, 1968, 221-234.

Records original publication of novels and foreign editions. Provides descriptions of production and contents of novels. Includes Singer's translations. Selective list of secondary items; coverage complements Item 486.

486. Bryer, Jackson R., and Paul E. Rockwell. "Isaac Bashevis Singer in English: A Bibliography." In *Critical Views of Isaac Bashevis Singer*. Ed. Irving Malin. New York: New York Univ. Press, 1969, 220-265.

Comprehensive checklist of Singer's published work in English records first American and English editions, reprintings of short works, and contents of collections. Annotation of secondary sources indicates scope and argument of items. Book reviews arranged by title of book. Coverage through June 1968.

487. Christensen, Bonniejean McGuire. "Isaac Bashevis Singer: A Bibliography." *Bulletin of Bibliography* 26.1 (January-March 1969): 3-6.

Enumerative checklist of works by and about Singer published from 1950 to 1968. Listing of short fiction is helpful for its alphabetical arrangement, but is not as complete as in Item 486.

488. Miller, David Neal. "A Bibliography of Isaac Bashevis Singer, January 1950-June 1952." Working Papers in Yiddish and East European Jewish Studies 34. New York: YIVO Institute for Jewish Research, 1979.

Records Yiddish-language books, contributions to newspapers, periodicals, translations, and anthology appearances by Singer. Also notes first publication of English translations of his work. Annotation for book titles only. Separate section records first periodical and book-form appearance of Singer's English-language writings. Comprehensive coverage is continued by Item 491.

489. Ryberg, Anders. "Bibliografi." In Knut Ahnlund's *Isaac Bashevis Singer: Hans sprak och hans varld*. Uppsala: Brombergs Bokforlag, 1979, 200-214.

> Coverage of primary works published in Yiddish and English into 1978. Lists book-length studies of Singer.

490. Hornbeck, David. "Isaac Bashevis Singer in the Last Ten Years." *Bulletin of Bibliography* 39.1 (March 1982): 17-25.

> Designed to fill gap between Item 487 and Singer's receipt of the Nobel Prize in October 1978. Covers English-language works by and about Singer.

491. Miller, David Neal. *Bibliography of Isaac Bashevis Singer, 1924-1949*. New York: Peter Lang, 1983.

> Comprehensive coverage reproduces format of Item 488. Suggests areas for further bibliographical research.

SLADEK, JOHN (1937-)

492. Drumm, Chris. *A John Sladek Checklist*. Polk City, Iowa: Chris Drumm, 1988.

> Provides a chronological enumerative listing of Sladek's writings. Identifies genre of each item and notes collaborations and reprintings. Many foreign-language editions are recorded, as are contents of his short story collections. Drumm states that this preliminary bibliography, with coverage to 1984, is based in part on a checklist supplied by Sladek.

SMITH, CORDWAINER (1915-)

493. Pierce, J.J. "Bibliography." In *Exploring Cordwainer Smith*. New York: Algol Press, 1975, 31-32.

Chronological record of Smith's published and unpublished science fiction through 1975. Excludes reprintings in magazines and anthologies.

SPENCER, ELIZABETH (1921-)

494. Barge, Laura. "An Elizabeth Spencer Checklist, 1948 to 1976." *Mississippi Quarterly* 29 (Fall 1976): 569-590.

Thorough coverage of works by Spencer and English-language commentary on her. Primary section lists Spencer's fiction (noting first British editions), contributions to periodicals (noting reprintings), and reviews. Secondary sources include review articles, interviews, book reviews, and theses. Treatment includes some foreign-language translations and critical studies.

SPENCER, SHARON (1933-)

495. "A Checklist of the Publications of Sharon Spencer." *Under the Sign of Pisces* 4.4 (Fall 1973): 9-10.

Provides an enumerative checklist of Spencer's fiction and literary criticism.

STAFFORD, JEAN (1915-1979)

496. Avila, Wanda. *Jean Stafford: A Comprehensive Bibliography*. Garland Reference Library of the Humanities 377. New York: Garland, 1983.

Near exhaustive coverage of primary materials includes monographs, stories, articles and essays, book and movie reviews, and miscellaneous statements, notes, recordings, and addresses. Provides printing information, noting first editions, paperback editions, foreign-language translations, and subsequent appearances of stories in anthologies and collections. Annotation summarizes Stafford's plots and critical arguments. Secondary section is divided into general criticism addressing two or more works, treatments of individual works (books or stories), foreign criticism, and doctoral dissertations. Entries are arranged alphabetically by author and unevenly annotated (foreign criticism is not annotated). Book reviews are grouped by title in order of publication; contents of the reviews are summarized. Other sections treat bio-bibliographical material; thorough coverage lists articles, reminiscences, interviews, and newspaper items dealing completely or in part with Stafford. Includes brief mentions and obituaries. Index allows access by title, author, and subject.

STONE, IRVING (1903-)

497. Stieg, Lewis F. *Irving Stone: A Bibliography*. Los Angeles: Friends of the Libraries of the Univ. of Southern California, 1973.

Enumerative checklist of books by Stone, with each entry followed by a listing of editions, foreign-language translations, condensations, excerpts, and adaptations. Records reviews and books edited by Stone, as well as his contributions to periodicals, anthologies, and other books. Coverage extends to 1970.

STONE, ROBERT (1937-)

498. Colonnese, Tom. "Robert Stone: A Working Checklist." *Bulletin of Bibliography* 39.3 (September 1982): 136-138.

Preliminary coverage of works by and about Stone through 1982. Primary and secondary sections arranged chronologically; contents drawn from standard indexes and databases.

STUART, JESSE (1907-1984)

499. Woodbridge, Hensley C. "Jesse Stuart: A Bibliographical Note." *American Book Collector* 9 (September 1958): 8-22.

Contains an enumerative checklist of books, stories, and translations of Stuart's works. Also summarizes arguments of unpublished theses. Accompanied by reproductions of dust jackets.

500. ----------. "Supplement to a Jesse Stuart Bibliography." *Bulletin of the Kentucky Library Association* 23 (January 1959): 9.

Records prefaces and short stories by Stuart through 1958 and omitted from Item 499.

501. ----------. "Jesse Stuart's Contributions to Newspapers." *Bulletin of the Kentucky Library Association* 23 (April 1959): 45-47.

Chronological coverage with items arranged by periodical in which they appeared. Lists poems, articles, editorials, and travel pieces. Woodbridge reports that this enumerative checklist constitutes the first attempt to collect these materials.

502. ----------. "Articles by Jesse Stuart: A Bibliography." *Bulletin of the Kentucky Library Association* 23 (July 1959): 89-91.

Records short stories, articles, and letters not listed in Item 499. Arrangement is alphabetical.

503. ----------. *Jesse Stuart: A Bibliography*. Harrogate, Tenn.: Lincoln Memorial Univ. Press, 1960.

Preliminary checklist of primary works through May 1960. Divided according to genre, books are arranged chronologically; stories, poems, and articles are listed alphabetically. Also includes letters, book reviews, anonymous contributions, and translations of Stuart's works. Coverage includes contents of collections, reprintings, condensations, and adaptations. Preface acknowledges that some original appearances of individual poems have not been identified. Revised as Item 506.

*504. ----------. "Jesse Stuart: A Bibliography for June 1960-May 1965." *Register of the Kentucky Historical Society* 63.4 (October 1965): 349-370.

According to the author in Item 505, this checklist reproduces the format of Item 503.

505. ----------. "Jesse Stuart: A Critical Bibliography." *American Book Collector* 16.6 (1966): 11-13.

A narrative survey that evaluates bibliographies, criticial and biographical studies, and other miscellaneous writings on Stuart.

506. ----------. *Jesse and Jane Stuart: A Bibliography*. Murray, Ky.: Murray State University, 1969.

Comprehensive treatment extends through 30 May 1969. Essentially reproduces format of Item 503 with the addition of 200 secondary sources.

507. ----------. "Jesse and Jane Stuart: A Bibliography, a Supplement for June-October 1969." *Jack London Newsletter* 2.3 (September-December 1969): 118-120. Continues under same title in subsequent issues through 8 (1975).

Registers works by Jane Stuart and writings by and about Jesse Stuart not listed in Item 506. Arranged by genre.

508. LeMaster, J. R. *Jesse Stuart: A Reference Guide*. Boston: G.K. Hall, 1979.

Enumerative coverage of principal primary works from 1934 to 1965. Thorough annotated secondary section extends to 1977 and is arranged chronologically.

509. ----------. *Jesse Stuart: Kentucky's Chronicler-Poet*. Memphis, Tenn.: Memphis State Univ. Press, 1980.

Expands coverage of primary works contained in Item 508.

STURGEON, THEODORE (1918-1985)

510. Moscowitz, Sam. "Fantasy and Science Fiction by Theodore Sturgeon (Bibliography)." *Magazine of Fantasy and Science Fiction* 23.2 (September 1962): 56-61.

Records first publications of Sturgeon's fantasy and science fiction works, distinguishing between first hardcover and first paperback editions. Lists only a few non-fantasy works by Sturgeon and only a few secondary items about him. Coverage to 1961. Superseded by Item 511.

511. Diskin, Lahna F. *Theodore Sturgeon: A Primary and Secondary Bibliography*. Boston: G.K. Hall, 1980.

Enumerates works by Sturgeon into 1977, including poetry, nonprint materials, book reviews and other nonfiction, and works edited. Notes reprintings of individual items. Annotated checklist of critical studies covers book reviews, articles, and essays. Well indexed.

STYRON, WILLIAM (1925-)

512. Schneider, Harold W. "Two Bibliographies: Saul Bellow, William Styron." *Critique* 3.3 (Summer 1960): 71-91, esp. 86-91.

Annotated checklist of works by and about Styron. Primary publications are arranged alphabetically by title, and include books, short stories, and articles. Some foreign-language editions and reprintings of individual items are noted. Secondary sources are comprised of biographical articles, book reviews, and articles.

513. Nigro, August J. "William Styron: Sélection bibliographique." *La Revue des Lettres Modernes* 157-161 (1967): 137-151. Reprinted in *William Styron*. Ed. Melvin Friedman and August J. Nigro. Configuration Critique 11. Paris: Minard, 1967, 137-151.

Provides an enumerative record of Styron's novels, articles, and reviews through 1966. Most useful for its listing of general studies, reviews, and essays on Styron published in French.

514. Bryer, Jackson R., and Marc Newman. "William Styron: A Bibliography." In *William Styron's 'The Confessions of Nat Turner': A Critical Handbook.* Ed. Melvin J. Friedman and Irving Malin. Belmont, Calif.: Wadsworth, 1970, 258-280.

Enumerative coverage of works by and about Styron to early 1969. Supplements and updates Items 512 and 513, with most thorough treatment reserved for critical responses to *The Confessions of Nat Turner.* Substantive book reviews are indicated.

515. Bryer, Jackson R. "William Styron: A Bibliography." In *The Achievement of William Styron.* Ed. Robert K. Morris and Irving Malin. Athens: Univ. of Georgia Press, 1975, 242-277; rev.ed. 1981.

Treats works by and about Styron through 1973. Enumerative primary section notes printing histories and lists recordings. Majority of secondary sources are from the 1960s and reviews of particularly noteworthy substance are indicated. Lists secondary materials not found in Item 516. Revised edition updates, corrects, and supplements earlier version, extending coverage to 1980. Section containing critical articles has been greatly expanded.

516. West, James L. III. *William Styron: A Descriptive Bibliography.* Boston: G.K. Hall, 1977.

Offers formal bibliographic descriptions of Styron's writings for the period 1938-1976. Annotations cover printing histories (including foreign translations) and describe patterns of textual transmission. Records Styron's ephemerae, juvenilia, published letters, and blurbs. Book covers are reproduced. General index.

517. Bryer, Jackson R., and Mary Beth Hatem. *William Styron: A Reference Guide.* Boston: G.K. Hall, 1978.

Records secondary sources for Styron published between 1946 and 1978. Separate sections treat book-length studies and shorter writings, arranged chronologically. Scope and argument of each item are briefly summarized. While treatment is comprehensive for English-language materials, coverage of foreign-language reviews and criticism is much more limited. Updates Item 515.

518. Leon, Philip W. *William Styron: An Annotated Bibliography of Criticism.* Westport, Ct.: Greenwood Press, 1978.

Offers detailed descriptions of works about Styron, including bibliographies, dissertations, and transient references. Entries summarize contents of critical works.

519. Bleikasten, André, and Jacques Pothier. "William Styron: Bibliographie Française." *Delta* 23 (October 1986): 175-186.

An enumerative listing of translations of Styron's books, articles, and extracts from his fiction published in French. Also records French interviews, general studies, and reviews of Styron's individual works.

SWANN, THOMAS BURNETT (1928-1976)

520. Collins, Robert A. "Thomas Burnett Swann: An Annotated Bibliography." In *Thomas Burnett Swann: A Brief Critical Biography and Annotated Bibliography.* Boca Raton: Florida Atlantic University Foundation, 1979, 19-29.

This chronological record of works by Swann parenthetically notes the genre of each item. Describes a variety of materials, including poems, stories, literary criticism, biography, articles, and novels by Swann. Often provides lengthy plot summaries for Swann's fiction. Collins states that his bibliography is not comprehensive, and suggests that the reader locate earlier bibliographic treatments by Robert A. Roehm which appeared in fanzines and which so far have proved impossible to locate.

TAYLOR, PETER (1917-)

521. Cathey, Kenneth C. "Peter Taylor: An Evaluation." *Western Review* 18.1 (Autumn 1953): 9-19, esp. 18-19.

    Coverage of Taylor's short stories, a play, and a novelette published before 1950. No secondary materials.

522. Smith, James Penny. "A Peter Taylor Checklist." *Critique* 9.3 (1967): 31-36.

    Records original publications, significant reprintings, and textbook appearances of Taylor's works. Also lists uncollected stories and works-in-progress. Secondary coverage includes theses, doctoral dissertations, and critical studies.

523. Kramer, Victor A., et al. *Andrew Lytle, Walker Percy, Peter Taylor: A Reference Guide.* Boston: G.K. Hall, 1983, esp. 189-243.

    Provides chronological record of writings about Taylor for the period 1948-1980. Treatment includes theses and dissertations, but consists primarily of book reviews.

THEROUX, PAUL (1941-)

524. Chaney, Bev. "Paul Theroux: A Bibliographical Checklist." *American Book Collector* ns 4.1 (January-February 1983): 30-37.

    Thorough coverage of Theroux's separately published works and his contributions to books into 1982. Provides physical descriptions and printing information. Treats Theroux's introductions, forewords, and published statements.

THOMPSON, JIM (1906-1977)

*525. "Bibliographie" for "Dossier Jim Thompson." *Polar* 2 (May 1979): 28-30.

Albert in Item 2 reports that this checklist records Thompson's first American publications and French translations.

*526. "Bibliography of Fiction." In *Jim Thompson: The Killers Inside Him*. Ed. Max Allan Collins and Ed Gorman. Cedar Rapids, Iowa: Fedora Press, 1983, 104.

A checklist of Thompson's twenty-nine books. Cited in Item 2.

TIPTREE, JAMES, JR. (1916-)

*527. "Tiptree/Sheldon Bibliography." *Khatru* 7 (1978): 23-25.

Listed in volume 2 of H. W. Hall's *Science Fiction and Fantasy Reference Index, 1878-1985: An International Author and Subject Index to History and Criticism* (Detroit: Gale Research, 1987).

528. Smith, Jeff. "James Tiptree, Jr. Bibliography." In Gardner Dozois, *The Fiction of James Tiptree, Jr*. San Bernardino, Calif.: Borgo Press, 1983, n.p.

Coverage of fiction and nonfiction arranged alphabetically, noting contents of collections, reprintings, and forthcoming works.

529. Siegel, Mark. "Primary Bibliography"; "Secondary Bibliography." In *James Tiptree, Jr*. Starmont Reader's Guide 22. Mercer Island, Wash.: Starmont House, 1985, 79-85; 86-87.

Provides enumerative treatment of works published under the names James Tiptree, Jr., Raccoona Sheldon, and Alice B. Sheldon. Annotations include plot summaries, title changes, and reprintings of individual items. Contents notes for secondary materials summarize argument and tone of each piece.

TRIMBLE, LOUIS (1917-)

530. "Bibliography of Louis Trimble's Works: Fiction Books and Academic Studies." In *English for Academic and Technical Purposes: Studies in Honor of Louis Trimble*. Ed. Larry Selinker, Elaine Tarone, and Victor Rowley. Rowley, Mass.: Newbury House Publishers, 1981, 225-227.

Enumerative list, arranged chronologically, of Trimble's fiction and nonfiction works published between 1938 and 1978.

TYLER, ANNE (1941-)

531. Nesanovich, Stella. "An Anne Tyler Checklist, 1959-1980." *Bulletin of Bibliography* 38.2 (April-June 1981): 53-64.

Complete chronological listing of published primary works. Notes editions, translations, and abridgements of novels; also records original and anthology appearances of stories. Limited coverage of secondary sources includes one doctoral dissertation and a variety of articles and book reviews.

532. Gardiner, Elaine, and Catherine Rainwater. "A Bibliography of Writings by Anne Tyler." In *Contemporary American Women Writers: Narrative Strategies*. Ed. Catherine Rainwater and William J. Scheick. Lexington: Univ. Press of Kentucky, 1985, 142-152.

While not as complete in its treatment as Item 531, this checklist is useful for updating Nesanovich's study to early 1984. Tyler's novels, stories, articles, and reviews are listed in separate sections.

UPDIKE, JOHN (1932-)

533. Taylor, C. Clarke. *John Updike: A Bibliography*. Serif Series 4. Kent, Ohio: Kent State Univ. Press, 1968.

Attempts comprehensive treatment of primary materials for the period 1949 to 1 July 1967. Works by Updike are arranged chronologically by genre and these entries are unannotated. Selection of secondary sources, including book reviews, articles, and critical studies, comprises a range of responses to Updike's work; each entry's scope and argument is summarized.

534. Sokoloff, B.A., and David E. Arnason. *John Updike: A Comprehensive Bibliography*. Folcroft, Pa.: Folcroft Press, 1971.

Comprehensive coverage extends into mid-1969. Treatment of primary texts notes subsequent publication of poems, as well as periodical and anthology appearances of stories and articles. Secondary sources are arranged chronologically and then alphabetically by reviewer or critic.

535. Meyer, Arlin G., and Michael A. Olivas. "Criticism of John Updike: A Selected Checklist." *Modern Fiction Studies* 20.1 (Spring 1974): 120-133.

Coverage spans the period 1960-1974. Selective record of secondary sources includes general studies, studies of individual works, and reviews. Excludes foreign criticism, minor reviews, and brief mentions of Updike. An additional feature is a list of Updike's then-uncollected essays, articles, reviews, and stories.

536. Olivas, Michael A. *An Annotated Bibliography of John Updike Criticism 1967-1973, and a Checklist of His Works*. Garland Reference Library of the Humanities 3. New York: Garland, 1975.

Lightly annotated primary section extends into 1974. Does not include original publications of subsequently collected material. Annotations of secondary sources are descriptive and occasionally evaluative. Supplements Item 535.

537. Gearhart, Elizabeth A. *John Updike: A Comprehensive Bibliography with Selected Annotations*. Norwood, Pa.: Norwood Editions, 1978.

Begun as a revision of Item 534, this checklist nearly doubles the number of entries found in Sokoloff's bibliography. Annotations in this treatment, however, are less thorough than those in Item 534. Arranges primary works by title and secondary sources by author. Reviews of Updike's books are not annotated.

538. Roberts, Ray A. "John Updike: A Bibliographical Checklist." *American Book Collector* ns 1.1 (January-February 1980): 5-12. Continued in *American Book Collector* ns 1.2 (March-April 1980): 39-47.

Records primary publications into 1979. Notes first U.S. and English editions and subsequent separate editions. Excludes periodical appearances. Part 2 lists Updike's other book appearances, including contributions to anthologies, forewords, responses to questionnaires, introductions, and translations. Detailed entries for all items.

539. Wright, Stuart. "John Updike's Contributions to *Chatterbox*." *Bulletin of Bibliography* 42.4 (December 1985): 171-178.

Enumerative checklist containing 285 items from the period 1945-1950. Treatment greatly expands previous records of Updike's juvenilia.

VANCE, JACK (1920-)

540. Briney, Robert. "Bibliography." In *Jack Vance: Science Fiction Stylist*. Ed. Richard Tiedman. Wabash, Ind.: Robert & Juanita Coulson, 1965, n.p.

Enumerative coverage limited to Vance's science fiction writings. Publication information for books includes series number, format, and price. Registers stories in science fiction magazines but does not list reprintings. Coverage to 1964.

541. Levack, Daniel J.H., and Tim Underwood. *Fantasms: A Bibliography of the Literature of Jack Vance*. San Francisco and Columbia, Pa.: Underwood-Miller, 1978.

Comprehensive listing of English-language works by Vance includes printing histories, anthology and collection appearances, works adapted for television, and items published in English-language periodicals through 1978. Treatment cross-references title changes, lists series and connected story sequences, and notes pseudonyms. Provides some physical descriptions and foreign-language book and periodical appearances when possible. Reproduces book covers and covers of magazines featuring Vance's stories. Includes chronological list of Vance's publications through early 1978.

542. Tymn, Marshall B. "Jack Vance: A Bibliography." In *Jack Vance*. Ed. Tim Underwood and Chuck Miller. New York: Taplinger, 1980, 227-234.

Enumerative alphabetical listings of books, pamphlets, short fiction, teleplays, and interviews with Vance. Selection of critical articles arranged alphabetically. Comprehensive coverage to 1979.

543. Curtis, Keith. "A Chronological Jack Vance Crime Checklist." *Science Fiction: A Review of Speculative Literature* 4.2 (June 1982): 79.

Enumerative record of books published from 1957 to 1979. Notes Vance's pseudonyms.

544. Levack, Daniel J.H. "Jack Vance: A Bibliography." *Science Fiction: A Review of Speculative Literature* 4.2 (June 1982): 82-84.

Treats Vance's novels, short stories, and nonprint materials, providing reprint information for his book-length works. Arrangement is alphabetical by title. Appends a list of general reference and critical sources.

VAN ITALLIE, JEAN-CLAUDE (1936-)

545. Brittain, Michael J. "A Checklist of Jean-Claude Van Itallie, 1961-1972." *Serif* 9.4 (Winter 1972): 75-77.

Enumerative checklist of works by Van Itallie. Records published plays and fiction (both original appearances and reprintings), television scripts (with broadcast dates), articles, and interviews.

VAN VOGT, A. E. (1912-)

546. Van Vogt, A. E. "Bibliography." In *Reflections of A. E. Van Vogt: The Autobiography of a Science Fiction Giant, with a Complete Bibliography*. Lakemont, Ga.: Fictioneer Books, 1975.

Van Vogt lists his science fiction publications in books, magazines, and anthologies, noting collaborations and some publication history. Coverage is limited to American editions.

547. Thiessen, Grant. "A.E. Van Vogt: A Brief Checklist." *Science Fiction Collector* 8 (October 1979): 7-22.

Enumerative checklist recording original hardcover and paperback editions of each novel and short story. Reprintings of these works are noted if titles changed from one printing to the next. Some anthology appearances have been included, especially if the stories are more accessible this way. Accompanied by reproductions of book covers.

VARLEY, JOHN (1947-)

*548. "John Varley: A Bibliography." *Digressions* 4 (February 1980): 17-18.

Cited in volume 2 of H. W. Hall's *Science Fiction and Fantasy Reference Index, 1878-1985: An International Author and Subject Index to History and Criticism* (Detroit: Gale Research, 1987).

549. Isajenko, Fred. "John Varley Bibliography." *Megavore* 12 (December 1980): 29-31.

An enumerative checklist of Varley's fiction and interviews. Contents notes describe reprintings of individual items, original serialization of book-length works, and stories found in his collections. Varley's award winning writings are indicated.

VIDAL, GORE (1925-)

550. Gilliam, Loretta Murrell. "Gore Vidal: A Checklist, 1945-1969." *Bulletin of Bibliography* 30.1 (January-March 1973): 1-9, 44.

Preliminary coverage of primary writings. Notes subsequent printings of individual items in anthologies and collections. Selective listing of secondary sources. Excludes translations and foreign-language newspaper and magazine appearances; does not treat miscellaneous items. Superseded by Item 551.

551. Stanton, Robert J. *Gore Vidal: A Primary and Secondary Bibliography*. Boston: G.K. Hall, 1978.

Fully descriptive annotations provide printing and revision histories of primary works, occasionally supplemented by Vidal's informal notes. Devotes sections to periodical appearances, manuscripts, translations, letters, and nonprint items. Thorough coverage of secondary sources allows tracing of Vidal as a fictional character in other writers' works and of his relationships with contemporary writers. Descriptive and evaluative annotations arranged chronologically. Introduction surveys Vidal's critical reception. Covers the period 1941-1978.

VIZENOR, GERALD ROBERT (1934-)

552. "Gerald Vizenor: A S.A.I.L. Bibliography #8." *Studies in American Indian Literature* 9.2 (Spring 1985): 46-49.

Provides an alphabetically arranged listing of Vizenor's book-length works, short fiction, and drama. Some entries are briefly annotated.

VONNEGUT, KURT, JR. (1922-)

553. Burns, Mildred Blair. "Books by Kurt Vonnegut." *Hollins Critic* 3.4 (October 1966): 7. Revised and expanded in *The Sounder Few: Selected Essays from The Hollins Critic.* Ed. R.H.W. Dillard. Athens: Univ. of Georgia Press, 1971, 192-193.

Enumerative list of books and subsequent editions. Coverage to 1966. Revised version extends coverage to 1969.

554. Schatt, Stanley, and Jerome Klinkowitz. "A Kurt Vonnegut Checklist." *Critique* 12.3 (1971): 70-76.

Enumerative record of primary writings accompanied by a selection of critical essays and reviews of Vonnegut's works. Coverage to 1970.

555. Hudgens, Betty. *Kurt Vonnegut, Jr.: A Checklist.* Detroit: Gale, 1972.

Intended as a preliminary checklist, coverage extends to mid-1972. Enumerative treatment of primary texts includes anthology appearances, juvenilia, interviews, dramatizations and screenplays based on Vonnegut's works, and blurbs written by Vonnegut. Notes subsequent publications and includes reproductions of title pages of first editions. Secondary section, which records early checklists and critical essays, is lightly annotated.

556. Klinkowitz, Jerome, Asa B. Pieratt, Jr., and Stanley Schatt. "The Vonnegut Bibliography." In *The Vonnegut Statement.* Ed. Jerome Klinkowitz and John Somer. New York: Delacorte Press/Seymour Lawrence, 1973, 255-277.

Thorough enumerative listing of works by and about Vonnegut. Primary coverage organized by type of material; secondary section includes foreign-language items and doctoral dissertations.

557. Pieratt, Asa B., Jr., and Jerome Klinkowitz. *Kurt Vonnegut, Jr.: A Descriptive Bibliography and Annotated Secondary Checklist.* Hamden, Ct.: Shoe String Press, 1974.

Coverage in primary section extends through late 1973. American, British, and foreign editions are noted, as are physical descriptions, printing histories, special editions, and variants in subsequent publications. Treats dramatic and cinematic adaptations of Vonnegut's works, recorded remarks and interviews, and collections of manuscripts and letters. Annotated secondary section divided into criticism, biography, book reviews, bibliographies and doctoral dissertations. Entries summarize critical arguments. Indexes list critics and primary works.

558. Haskell, John D., Jr. "Addendum to Pieratt and Klinkowitz: Kurt Vonnegut, Jr." *Papers of the Bibliographic Society of America* 70.1 (January-March 1976): 122.

Verifies the existence of a short story not listed in Item 557.

559. Lercangée, Francine. *Kurt Vonnegut, Jr.: A Selected Bibliography.* Brussels: Center for American Studies, 1976.

Emphasis is on secondary materials culled from newspapers, journals, magazines, books, and theses. With enumerative coverage to 1973, most items have been included in subsequent bibliographies.

560. Klinkowitz, Jerome. "The Vonnegut Bibliography." In *Vonnegut in America: An Introduction to the Life and Work of Kurt Vonnegut.* Ed. Jerome Klinkowitz and Donald J. Lawler. New York: Dell, 1977, 217-252.

Reproduces format of Item 556 with coverage to late 1976.

561. Pieratt, Asa B., Jr., Julie Huffman-Klinkowitz, and Jerome Klinkowitz. *Kurt Vonnegut: A Comprehensive Bibliography.* Hamden, Ct.: Shoe String Press, 1987.

> Thorough coverage of works by and about Vonnegut through October 1985. Notes corrections and emendations of Item 557, along with sections listing Vonnegut's tape and film appearances, and collected works. Doubles the number of secondary citations and provides four times the number of doctoral dissertations noted in Item 557.

WALKER, ALICE (1944-)

562. Kirschner, Susan. "Alice Walker's Nonfictional Prose: A Checklist, 1966-1984." *Black American Literature Forum* 18.4 (Winter 1984): 162-163.

> Arranged generically, this enumerative checklist records Walker's essays, published lectures, reviews, interviews, letters, and miscellaneous writings. Coverage is through early 1984.

563. Pratt, Louis H., and Darnell D. Pratt. *Alice Malsenior Walker: An Annotated Bibliography: 1968-1986.* Meckler's Studies and Bibliographies on Black Americans 1. Westport, Ct.: Meckler, 1988.

> Enumerative coverage of primary works includes Walker's collections, recordings, and uncollected materials, while deliberately omitting anthology appearances. Thorough treatment of secondary sources.

WALLANT, EDWARD LEWIS (1926-1962)

564. Ayo, Nicholas. "Edward Lewis Wallant, 1926-1962." *Bulletin of Bibliography* 28.4 (October-December 1971): 119.

Enumerative checklist of works by Wallant, including a variety of unpublished materials. Also records a list of critical articles about Wallant.

WALSH, THOMAS (1908-1984)

*565. Lachman, Marvin. "Department of Unknown Mystery Writers: Thomas Walsh." *Poisoned Pen* 2.1 (January-February 1979): 15-19.

Recorded by Albert in Item 2.

WALTON, EVANGELINE (1907-)

566. Zahorski, Kenneth J., and Robert Boyer. *Lloyd Alexander, Evangeline Walton Ensley, Kenneth Morris: A Primary and Secondary Bibliography*. Boston: G.K. Hall, 1981, esp. 113-159.

Fiction and nonfiction are arranged chronologically and listed enumeratively. Records subsequent reprintings and some foreign-language editions. Contents notes for secondary items are both descriptive and evaluative. Coverage in both sections is to 1980.

WARREN, ROBERT PENN (1905-)

567. Beebe, Maurice, and Erin Marcus. "Criticism of Robert Penn Warren: A Selected Checklist." *Modern Fiction Studies* 6.1 (Spring 1960): 83-88.

Enumerative treatment of general studies and works dealing primarily with either Warren's poetry or his fiction. Superseded by later listings of secondary sources.

568. Casper, Leonard. "The Works of Robert Penn Warren: A Chronological Checklist." In *Robert Penn Warren: The Dark and Bloody Ground*. Seattle: Univ. of Washington Press, 1960, 191-200.

Enumerative primary and secondary coverage through late 1959. A thorough treatment that includes textbooks and anthologies edited by Warren, excerpts, and short fiction. Secondary items are arranged alphabetically by author. Contained in the first book-length study of Warren, this bibliography is often cited as an important source for later bibliographic treatments.

569. Huff, Mary Nance. *Robert Penn Warren: A Bibliography*. New York: David Lewis, 1968.

Primary and secondary coverage of the period 1923-1968. Books arranged chronologically, stories and poems alphabetically. Thorough enumerative treatment cites printing histories of individual works, including translations, and nonprint items. Limited coverage of secondary materials is lightly annotated and relies heavily on previously published checklists.

*570. Grimshaw, James A., Jr. "Robert Penn Warren: A Bibliographical Catalogue, Being a Description of His First American Editions Printed through 31 December 1971, along with Individual Titles, an Annotated Checklist of Secondary Sources, and an Index." Ph.D. Diss. Louisiana State Univ., 1972.

Dissertation Abstracts International 33 (1972): 2375A reports that this bibliography provides comprehensive coverage of works by and about Warren.

571. ----------. "Robert Penn Warren's *All the King's Men*: An Annotated Checklist of Criticism." *Resources for American Literary Study* 6.1 (Spring 1976): 23-69.

Records the reviews, review articles, and critical studies of *All the King's Men* published between August 1946 and December 1972. Arrangement is chronological and entries' contents are briefly summarized.

572. Nakadate, Neil. *Robert Penn Warren: A Reference Guide*. Boston: G.K. Hall, 1977.

Intended as a comprehensive treatment of all significant scholarship devoted to Warren over the period 1925-1975. Items treated include monographs, critical essays and articles, and reviews in quarterly journals and major newspapers. Notations give scope, content, and argument of each item. Includes some foreign materials, indicating items not seen. Arrangement is chronological by year, then alphabetical by author. Well indexed.

573. Grimshaw, James A., Jr. *Robert Penn Warren: A Descriptive Bibliography 1922-1979*. Published for the Bibliographical Society of America. Charlottesville: Univ. Press of Virginia, 1981.

Detailed treatment of primary materials includes physical descriptions, accounts of revisions, and summaries of contents. Separate sections list manuscript holdings, foreign translations, collaborations, and awards and recognitions. Additional sections describe works set to music, audiovisual presentations, tributes to, and recordings by Warren. Secondary sources, among them checklists of criticism and unpublished studies, are covered through late 1979. Thorough indexes are arranged by name, title, and subject.

WATERS, FRANK (1902-)

574. Lyon, Thomas J. *Frank Waters*. Twayne's United States Author Series 225. New York: Twayne, 1973.

Selective enumerative list of works by and about Waters into 1969. Materials treated include short reviews, nonfiction, and newspaper editorials. Some subsequent printings noted. Limited list of secondary sources lightly annotated. Still valuable for its treatment of criticism on Waters.

575. Tanner, Terence A. *Frank Waters: A Bibliography, with Relevant Selections from His Correspondence*. Glenwood, Ill.: Meyerbooks, 1983.

Comprehensive coverage spans the period 1916-1981. Descriptive annotations, based in part on Waters's own files, are provided for his broadsides, juvenilia, journalism, pamphlets, and dust jacket blurbs. Treatment notes periodical and anthology appearances, printing histories of individual items, and original publication of materials contributed to other writers' works. Contents of collections are listed for the each book's earliest printing. Notes translations of Waters's writings. Selective secondary section is arranged alphabetically by author and includes book reviews, dissertations, and some criticism.

WELLMAN, MANLY WADE (1903-1986)

*576. Benson, Gordon, Jr. *Manly Wade Wellman: The Gentleman from Chapel Hill*. Albuquerque: Gordon Benson, 1986.

A working bibliography that is not intended to be complete. Described in Marshall B. Tymn, "The Year's Scholarship in Fantastic Literature: 1986." *Extrapolation* 28.3 (Fall 1987): 201-254.

WELTY, EUDORA (1909-)

577. Smythe, Katherine Hinds. "Eudora Welty: A Checklist." *Bulletin of Bibliography* 21.9 (January-April 1956): 207-208.

Unannotated coverage of primary works through July 1954. Notes changes in short story titles, reprintings of books, and translations. Excludes book reviews and anthology appearances. Contents of collections are recorded.

578. Gross, Seymour. *Secretary's News Sheet* (Bibliographical Society of Virginia) 40 (April 1960): 1-32.

The first comprehensive attempt at a bibliography of Welty's writings. Treats newspaper items, textbook explications of her stories, and Welty's published comments on her own writing. Covers the period 1936-1955.

579. Jordan, Leona. "Eudora Welty: Selected Criticism." *Bulletin of Bibliography* 23.1 (January-April 1960): 14-15.

     Based on standard indexes and previously published bibliographies.

580. Cole, McKelva. "Eudora Welty's Book Reviews." *Bulletin of Bibliography* 23.10 (January-April 1963): 240.

     Enumerative record of reviews by Welty published between 1943 and 1961, arranged chronologically.

581. McDonald, W. U., Jr. "Eudora Welty Manuscripts: An Annotated Finding List." *Bulletin of Bibliography* 24.2 (September-December 1963): 44-46.

     Describes subject matter and significance of letters and manuscripts as well as indicating their location.

582. Polk, Noel. "A Eudora Welty Checklist." *Mississippi Quarterly* 26.4 (Fall 1973): 663-693.

     Descriptive treatment of primary works, including book reviews, interviews, poems, and photographs. Notes subsequent publication of individual items. List of secondary works includes all full-length studies of aspects of Welty's work, a sampling of contemporary reviews of her books as they were published, and only the most useful textbook explications of individual stories. Expanded into Item 591.

583. McDonald, W.U., Jr. "Eudora Welty Manuscripts: A Supplementary Annotated Finding List." *Bulletin of Bibliography* 31.3 (July-September 1974): 95-98, 126, 132.

     Supplements and updates coverage of Item 581 to 1962.

584. Thompson, Victor H. *Eudora Welty: A Reference Guide*. Boston: G.K. Hall, 1976.

Chronological coverage of secondary materials extends into 1975. Entries arranged alphabetically by author within each year. Treats textbook explications and newspaper items; record of Welty's own writing includes her literary criticism but excludes her book reviews. Annotations summarize critical argument of individual entries.

585. Blayac, Alain. "The Eudora Welty Collection at the Humanities Research Center, the University of Texas at Austin." *Delta* 5 (November 1977): 83-88.

Lists the manuscripts, correspondence, and first or special editions housed in this collection. Some physical descriptions of individual items are provided.

586. *Eudora Welty Newsletter* 1.1- (Winter 1977-).

Issued twice a year, this ongoing newsletter devotes itself principally to bibliographical matters. Regular features include continuing checklists of Welty's newly published work, of recent Welty scholarship and reviews, and of articles about her in regional sources, especially local newspapers. Occasional articles address various topics in the descriptive bibliography of her writings, including textual variants, the publishing histories of individual titles, and her contribution of publicity blurbs to other writers' works. Censuses of Welty's manuscripts in public repositories are also routinely printed. Serves to expand and update book-length bibliographic studies of Welty.

587. Polk, Noel. "Eudora Welty: A Bibliographical Checklist." *American Book Collector* ns 2.1 (January-February 1981): 25-37.

Briefly describes first American and English editions as well as subsequent issues of books. Also records forty other primary items, including photographs, stories, tributes to other writers, speeches, comments on her own work, interviews, and responses to questionnaires. Detailed annotation for all items.

588. Swearingen, Bethany C. *Eudora Welty: A Critical Bibliography, 1936-1958*. Jackson: Univ. Press of Mississippi, 1984.

Intended to provide very complete coverage of the first twenty years of Welty's literary career. Enumerative primary section notes first appearances of individual stories and their subsequent publication. Summarizes contents of her essays and articles. Superseded by Item 591 except that stories here are arranged alphabetically. Secondary section is divided into general criticism, studies of individual works, and selected references to local materials on Welty. Selective coverage is generously annotated with summaries of critical arguments, which complement Item 591.

589. Marrs, Suzanne. "An Annotated Bibliography of the *Losing-Battles* Papers." *Southern Quarterly* 23.2 (Winter 1985): 116-121.

Chronological listing of manuscript materials held by the Mississippi Department of Archives and History.

590. McHaney, Pearl Amelia. "A Eudora Welty Checklist, 1973-1986." In *Welty: A Life in Literature*. Ed. Albert J. Devlin. Jackson: Univ. Press of Mississippi, 1987, 266-302.

Designed to supplement Item 591. Notes that reprint histories, foreign-language translations, and blurbs by Welty have been excluded. Secondary section restricted to items making a significant contribution to Welty scholarship.

591. Polk, Noel. "A Eudora Welty Checklist, 1936-1972." In *Welty: A Life in Literature*. Ed. Albert J. Devlin. Jackson: Univ. Press of Mississippi, 1987, 238-265.

Updates and offers corrections to Item 582. Coverage actually extends into 1973. Together with Item 590 provides fairly thorough survey of Welty's career and critical reception.

592. Vande Kieft, Ruth M. "Selected Bibliography." In *Eudora Welty*. Rev. ed. Twayne's United States Authors Series 15. New York: Twayne, 1987, 203-206. 1st ed. 1962.

Coverage of primary and secondary sources to 1986. Noteworthy for its list of film appearances by Welty.

WEST, JESSAMYN (1902-1984)

593. Shivers, Alfred S. "Jessamyn West." *Bulletin of Bibliography* 28.1 (January-March 1971): 1-3.

First attempt at a comprehensive checklist of works by West. Sections record books, uncollected poems and stories, and articles, speeches, and introductions. Contains a selective list of articles about West. Unannotated coverage to early 1970.

WESTLAKE, DONALD E. (1933-)

594. Kodata, Nobumitsu, and Donald E. Westlake. "Donald E. Westlake: A Checklist." *Armchair Detective* 8 (1974-1975): 203-205; McSherry, Frank D., Jr. "Addendum." *Armchair Detective* 8 (1974-1975): 319.

Provides a chronological record of Westlake's writings as Donald E. Westlake, Richard Stark, and Tucker Coe, treating book-length works published between 1960 and 1975, and short stories and articles from the period 1954-1973. The addendum verifies the existence of a short story that was missed in the checklist.

595. Naudon, Jean-François. "Bibliographie de Donald Westlake." *Polar* 22 (15 January 1982): 45-58.

Arranged by date of publication, this checklist of Westlake's books records first American editions, French translations, and reprintings of French editions. Also lists short stories that have been translated into French. Accompanied by still photographs from film adaptations of Westlake's works.

596. Schleret, Jean-Jacques. "Filmographie commentée de Donald Westlake." *Polar* 22 (15 January 1982): 60-68.

Treats film adaptations of Westlake's novels, giving French and American titles whenever possible, and accompanied by often lengthy remarks from Westlake. The checklist includes screenplays by Westlake that are not based on his own fiction, as well as his movie projects that were aborted.

*597. "Attempt at a Bibliography." *The ParkerPhile*. St. Paul, Minn.: Coe-Stark Associates, 1982-1983.

Albert in Item 2 reports that this irregularly published fanzine contains biographical, bibliographical, and critical material on Westlake and his pseudonyms. "Attempt at a Bibliography" appeared in four installments.

WHITTINGTON, HARRY (1915-)

*598. "Harry Whittington: Bibliographie chronologique" and "Harry Whittington: Filmographie." *Les Amis du crime* 5 (March 1980): 17-29, 30-33.

The filmography lists movie and television adaptations of Whittington's fiction. The checklist records books and short stories, including reprintings and some French translations. Described by Albert in Item 2.

WIESEL, ELIE (1928-)

599. Abramowitz, Molly. *Elie Wiesel: A Bibliography*. Scarecrow Author Bibliographies 22. Metuchen, N.J.: Scarecrow Press, 1974.

Attempts to cover works by and about Wiesel into 1974. Provides fairly complete treatment of English-language materials, but is more selective in coverage of works in French, Hebrew, and Yiddish. Deliberately excludes Wiesel's correspondent work and published radio, television, and movie scripts. Notes contents of collections and summarizes plots and arguments of Wiesel's stories, reviews, and critical pieces. The author cites her sometimes arbitrary distinction between Wiesel's fiction and nonfiction. Arranged alphabetically by author, secondary sources include critical essays, interviews, doctoral dissertations, reviews of English-language editions, and reviews of foreign-language editions.

WILLIAMS, JOHN (1922-)

600. Dayal, Samir, and Tandy Sturgeon. "John Williams: A Bibliography." *Denver Quarterly* 20.3 (Winter 1986): 147-154.

Enumerative record of works by and about Williams. Primary section lists novels, poetry, short fiction, essays, and editorial work. Chronological arrangement, with reprintings of individual items omitted. Includes a selection of reviews, critical studies, and general bio-bibliographical sources.

WILLIAMS, JOHN A. (1925-)

601. Muller, Gilbert H. *John A. Williams*. Twayne's United States Authors Series 472. Boston: Twayne, 1984.

Selective coverage of fiction, nonfiction, interviews, and uncollected articles and essays into 1982. Deliberately selective secondary section provides evaluative descriptions and summaries of critical commentary on Williams.

WILLIAMSON, JACK (1908-)

602. Myers, Robert E. *Jack Williamson: A Primary and Secondary Bibliography*. Boston, G.K. Hall, 1980.

Comprehensive primary section arranged chronologically by type of material, including fiction, nonfiction, and miscellaneous media. Enumerative treatment lists subsequent printings and foreign-language editions of Williamson's work, for which Myers draws on his library, and Williamson's own collection and informal notes. Appendices organize reviews of Williamson's work by individual title, and alphabetically by author. Provides contents notes for secondary sources.

603. Luserke, Uwe. "Jack Williamson Bibliography." *Megavore* 13 (March 1981): 29-41.

Chronological enumerative listing of first printings of Williamson's individual stories and novels. Notes twelve items available only in their original format. Reproductions of book covers supplement coverage. Corrects errors contained in Item 602.

WILSON, RICHARD (1920-)

*604. Drumm, Chris. *A Richard Wilson Checklist/Adventures in the Space Trade: A Memoir by Richard Wilson*. Polk City, Iowa: Chris Drumm, 1986.

While not seen, this bibliography is listed in Marshall B. Tymn's "The Year's Scholarship in Fantastic Literature: 1986." *Extrapolation* 28.3 (Fall 1987): 201-254. Tymn describes the checklist as covering the period 1940-1986.

WOLFE, BERNARD (1915-1985)

605. Geduld, Carolyn. *Bernard Wolfe*. Twayne's United States Authors Series 211. New York: Twayne, 1972.

Selective coverage of primary works through 1968. Entries are arranged chronologically by type of material. Lightly annotated treatment includes separately published chapters of novels, uncollected essays, journalism, television scripts, and books ghostwritten for Wolfe. More limited secondary section focuses on book reviews and characterizes the reactions of individual reviewers as positive or negative.

WOLFE, GENE (1931-)

606. Benson, Gordon, Jr. "Gene Rodman Wolfe: A Bio-Bibliography." In Gene Wolfe, *The Castle of the Otter*. Willimantic, Ct.: Ziesing Brothers, 1982, 104-113.

Enumerative checklist of works through 1981, with some items from 1982-83. Lists stories in order of sale (and notes subsequent printings); books are arranged in order of publication. Treats translations of Wolfe's books. Based in large part on standard indexes and databases.

607. Nelson, Chris. "Books by Gene Wolfe: A Checklist." *Science Fiction: A Review of Speculative Literature* 7.1 (1985): 15-17.

Lists Wolfe's books alphabetically by title, recording American and British editions. Treatment notes contents of short story collections, as well as pagination and prices of individual items.

608. Gordon, Joan. "Complete Annotated Bibliography of Fiction Cited by First Editions"; "Selected and Annotated Bibliography of Non-Fiction Writing"; "Selected and Annotated Secondary Bibliography." In *Gene Wolfe*. Starmont Reader's Guide 29. San Bernardino, Calif.: Borgo Press, 1986, 100-107; 108; 109-110.

Fiction and nonfiction are arranged alphabetically, while interviews and critical articles are listed by author. Useful for the descriptions that accompany all entries.

YERBY, FRANK (1916-)

609. Hill, James Lee. "Bibliography of the Writings of Chester Himes, Ann Petry and Frank Yerby." *Black Books Bulletin* 3.3 (1975): 60-72, esp.69-72.

An enumerative record of Yerby's writings, supplemented by a list of biographical and critical articles about him.

ZEBROWSKI, GEORGE (1945-)

610. Elliot, Jeffrey M., and R. Reginald. *The Work of George Zebrowski: An Annotated Bibliography & Guide*. Bibliographies of Modern Authors 4. San Bernardino, Calif.: Borgo Press, 1986.

Offers comprehensive coverage of Zebrowski's career through 1985. Sections arranged generically. Annotation provides a plot summary and printing history of individual items (especially short stories). Zebrowski's juvenilia, editing of fanzines, honors and awards, and public appearances are chronicled. Unpublished and forthcoming works, manuscripts, and translations of Zebrowski's works are also listed. Lightly annotated secondary section.

ZELAZNY, ROGER (1937-)

611. Curtis, Keith. "Roger Zelazny: A Selected Checklist." *Science Fiction: A Review of Speculative Literature* 1.2 (June 1978): 25-26.

Covers the period 1965-1978, listing first U.S. and British editions of Zelazny's books. Notes contents of short story collections and collaborations.

612. Sanders, Joseph L. *Roger Zelazny: A Primary and Secondary Bibliography*. Boston: G.K. Hall, 1980.

A thorough account of primary materials (including poetry and nonfiction) through late 1979. Descriptions note printing histories of all works and often include remarks by Zelazny. Secondary section lists and annotates major studies, reviews, and brief references to Zelazny's work. Provides a biographical sketch and overview of Zelazny's critical reception. Appendices list nominations, awards, and honors, as well as foreign-language editions, manuscripts, and papers. Separate indexes for primary and secondary sources.

613. Levack, Daniel J. H. *Amber Dreams: A Roger Zelazny Bibliography*. San Francisco and Columbia, Pa.: Underwood-Miller, 1983.

Attempts an exhaustive record of all published works of fiction through late 1982. Provides physical descriptions, analyses of content, and photographs of book covers. Includes previously published annotations by Zelazny and printing histories. Introduction notes that some foreign-language editions may not have been included; published letters and book reviews by Zelazny have been deliberately omitted. Additional sections list pseudonymous appearances and collaborations. Indexes trace verse and nonfiction. Provides a chronological list of publications. Supplements and updates Item 612.

Subject Index

Names appearing as subjects are listed in their most widely recognized form. Index numbers refer to entries, not pages.

Author Index

Index numbers refer to entries, not pages.

Dworkin, Rita, 1

Eger, Ernestina N., 15
Elliot, Jeffrey M., 610
Elwood, Roger, 397, 399
Engebretson, David, 299
Engeldinger, Eugene A., 18
Eppard, Philip B., 6
Erisman, Fred, 16
Eschholz, Paul A., 36
Espley, John L., 435
Etulain, Richard W., 16, 255

Fabre, Michel, 216, 275
Fagerheim, Cynthia, 438
Fairbanks, Carol, 18; *see also*
  Myers, Carol Fairbanks
Fallon, Eileen, 17
Farmer, David R., 415
Field, Andrew, 371, 372
Field, Kathleen, 355
Field, Leslie, 103
Fiene, Donald M., 467, 468
Fikes, Robert, Jr., 361, 367, 460
Fischer, Russell G., 75
Flanagan, Graeme, 115
Flora, Joseph M., 19
Flynn, George, 462
Fox, Hugh, 143
Frane, Jeff, 315
Franklin, Benjamin, V., 382, 383,
  385
Franklin, H. Bruce, 267
French, Ned, 242
Friedman, Melvin J., 407, 513, 514

Gale, Steven H., 431, 432
Gann, Daniel H., 173, 427
Gardiner, Elaine, 532

Gargan, William, 289, 290
Garon, Paul, 58
Garrett, George, 237
Gaston, Edwin W., Jr., 3
Gearhart, Elizabeth A., 537
Geduld, Carolyn, 605
Getz, Lorine M., 414, 416
Gildzen, Alex, 362
Gillespie, Bruce, 192
Gilliam, Loretta Murrell, 550
Giza, Joanne, 220
Golden, Robert E., 413
Goldman, Sherli Evens, 347
Goodman, Michael B., 146
Gordon, Joan, 608
Gorman, Ed, 526
Graham, Ronald E., 150
Grant, Richard, 178
Grau, Joseph A., 336
Greenberg, Martin Harry, 70, 130,
  194, 310
Gretlund, Jan Nordby, 285
Grimm, Clyde L., Jr., 249, 250
Grimshaw, James A., Jr., 570, 571,
  573
Grissom, Margaret S., 252
Gross, Seymour, 578
Guzlowski, John Z., 103

Habich, Robert D., 335
Hagen, Lyman B., 134
Hall, Blaine H., 105
Hall, Graham M., 112
Hall, H.W., 418
Hamilton, Lee T., 235
Hansen, Elaine Tuttle, 434
Hargraves, Michael, 172, 174, 248
Harris, Trudier, 11, 12
Haskell, John D., Jr., 558

Rowell, Charles H., 232
Rowley, Victor, 530
Rubin, Louis D., Jr., 37
Ruoff, Lavonne Brown, 419
Rusch, Frederic E., 303
Rush, Theresa Gunnels, 38
Rushing, Lynda Lee, 144
Ryberg, Anders, 489

Sadoya, Shigenobu, 328
Salzberg, Joel, 337
Sanders, Joseph L., 612
Schatt, Stanley, 554, 556
Scheick, William J., 92, 199, 420, 423, 434, 458, 532
Schleifer, Ronald, 423
Schleret, Jean-Jacques, 136, 139, 171, 286, 596
Schlobin, Roger C., 39, 42, 46, 315, 401
Schmidt, Dorey, 360
Schneider, Duane, 385
Schneider, Harold W., 98, 512
Schuman, Samuel, 374
Schweig, Jean-Paul, 286
Schweyer, Janine, 348
Scotto, Robert M., 262, 270, 453
Selinker, Larry, 530
Settle, Elizabeth A., 459, 461
Settle, Robert A., 459, 461
Shapiro, Adrian M., 354, 355
Shepard, Douglas H., 327
Sher, Morris, 333
Shine, Jean, 319
Shine, Walter, 319
Shivers, Alfred S., 593
Siegel, Mark, 529
Simon, Renee B., 437
Skerl, Jennie, 145

Skinner, Robert F., 322
Smith, Curtis C., 40
Smith, James Penny, 522
Smith, Jeff, 528
Smith, Myron J., Jr., 41
Smythe, Katherine Hinds, 577
Snodgrass, Kathleen, 149
Sokoloff, B.A., 99, 324, 534
Sola, Graciela de, 229
Somer, John, 556
Staicar, Tom, 316
Standley, Fred L., 76, 81
Standley, Nancy V., 81
Stanley, William T., 351
Stanton, Robert J., 156, 551
Starosciak, Kenneth, 154, 469
Stewart, Stanley, 349
Stieg, Lewis F., 497
Straayer, T.A., 189
Studing, Richard, 57
Sturgeon, Tandy, 600
Sublette, Jack, 471
Sullivan, Mary C., 413
Surdi, Alessandra Pinto, 35
Swearingen, Bethany C., 588
Swigart, Leslie Kay, 211, 212

Tanner, Terence A., 575
Tarone, Elaine, 530
Taylor, C. Clarke, 533
Thiessen, Grant, 547
Thompson, Raymond H., 196
Thompson, Victor H., 584
Tiedman, Richard, 540
Trakas, Deno, 160
Trujillo, Roberto G., 43
Tuck, Donald H., 44, 150, 479
Turner, David G., 398

.